Carol Klein's Favourite Plants

Choosing & growing plants by character

Photographs by Jonathan Buckley
Edited by Erica Hunningher

MITCHELL BEAZLEY

To my Mum, Jeannie,
who sowed the first seeds of all this

Carol Klein's Favourite Plants

First published in Great Britain in 2004
as *Plant Personalities* by Cassell Illustrated.
This edition published in 2012 by Mitchell Beazley,
a division of Octopus Publishing Group Limited,
Endeavour House, 189 Shaftesbury Avenue,
London, WC2H 8JY
www.octopusbooks.co.uk

An Hachette UK Company
www.hachette.co.uk

ISBN 978 1 84533 705 6

A CIP record for this book is available from the British Library
Set in Chronicle Deck
Printed and bound in China

For this edition:
Publisher: Alison Starling
Art Director: Jonathan Christie
Assistant Editor: Stephanie Milner
Production Controller: Sarah Kramer

Half title
Erythronium hendersonii, a North American trout lily, reflexes
its petals seductively in its spring display. By summer it has gone
to ground.

Title page
This foxglove seedling *(Digitalis)* arrived by chance. Some of the
best plants are uninvited guests.

Opposite
Pulsatilla vulgaris, one of the softest touches of the plant world.

Contents

Introduction

THIS IS A BRAND-NEW EDITION OF MY FIRST BOOK. Since I wrote it, I've had the opportunity to share my affection for many of the plants within its pages with viewers of 'Gardeners World,' several 'specials' and the six-part series 'Life in a Cottage Garden,' filmed in my garden in North Devon, Glebe Cottage.

I've come to know intimately most of the plants within these pages by growing them both in my garden and in the nursery I've run for more than thirty years. The great majority are hardy herbaceous perennials with a sprinkling of bulbs. I love herbaceous plants. The way they change and develop throughout the seasons makes garden life exciting at every twist and turn: every day new pictures unfold as shoots lengthen, buds swell and flowers burst. There is beautiful foliage and there are seed heads and often autumn colour.

Plants can be entertaining too. Some of them are funny. They can be cheeky and provocative, shy and retiring or flamboyant and voluptuous. We may think we choose plants for their height or habit, or for the colour of their flowers, no doubt we do, but they are much more than a collection of physical characteristics. Sometimes there is something so engaging about a plant that we feel we just have to grow it.

Getting close to plants, understanding their needs and trying to ensure that they have the best conditions in which to thrive, is a privilege. Enabling them to be themselves and develop their true characters is a labour of love. The longer we grow plants, the better we get to know them. The more closely we are acquainted, the more aware we become of their individuality, their quirks and eccentricities and, most importantly, the essential qualities which make them what they are – or who they are.

Do plants really have personalities? I have been growing the plants we feature in this book for many years here at Glebe Cottage. The more intimately I get to know them, the more I am struck by their individuality, and yet how they often share qualities with plants to which they are botanically unrelated. In the volumes written about plants, they are classified according to the plant family to which they belong, or they are grouped for seasonal interest, colour, hardiness rating or other attributes. All these factors and especially a plant's suitability for different conditions are important, and I have tried to give as much information as possible about each of the plants that appear which I hope will help anyone trying to grow them for the first time. Although this is not a 'how to' book I've tried to pass on any experience I've had growing these plants. Primarily, however, I consider each plant as a personality, with traits which place it fairly and squarely with others in its chapter.

Looking at plants in personality groups does not purport to be a scientific system, but it is an entertaining way of appreciating them and an informative way of rating the contribution they make to the garden. Whether a Cinderella who shoots to stardom before the clock strikes twelve or a Drama Queen who grabs all our attention, the plants themselves dictated the names of each group. All are plants which I care for and although it is true to say that I need no excuse to discuss them *ad infinitum*, writing this book has allowed me to share my observations.

Gardening is not just an opportunity to get our hands in the soil. For many of us it is our only chance to create something of our own. The only limitations are physical – how much space have we got, what are our soil and weather like and which way does our plot face? The rest is up to us and we all do it differently. We all have our plant preferences, but even when we use the same plants we put them together in our own way.

Since its inception, this book has been a collaboration. Jonathan's pictures are as important as my words in developing these ideas about plant personalities. Almost all his photographs were taken at Glebe Cottage. His photography closes the gap between gardener and plant, allowing us unprecedented access to its most intimate nature. His pictures provide a refreshingly accessible perspective. Thinking about plants as personalities has broadened our outlook. Rather than blinkering vision and inhibiting plant choice, it allows us more freedom – and helps us to have much more fun.

Carol Klein

1.

Cinderella plants

Left
Springtime and the first Cinderellas – wood anemones and snakeshead fritillaries – thrust their way through the dark earth, embroidering a vital tapestry. The rosettes of Primula japonica *unfurl prior to launching their flowers.*

Cinderella plants shoot to stardom in a matter of weeks, accomplishing their whole cycle – flowering, pollination, setting seed – then disappearing into dormancy before the clock strikes twelve. If you listen closely enough you can almost hear the quiet groaning of the leafy earth as the spears of snowdrops split it apart, thrusting their grey-green shoots ever upwards. The restless rustling of wood anemones follows as they wriggle from side to side, striving to push their lacy shoulders through the sodden soil, their arms folded tightly around their infant buds. This fleeting performance is typical of spring flowers, especially those whose stage is the woodland floor. When the canopy fills in overhead, it deprives carpeting plants of light and water and forces them into hibernation until next spring. Then their reappearance reassures and simultaneously excites yet again, offering a mouth-watering taste of thrills to come.

THE SIGHT OF SNOWDROP SHOOTS pushing through the sleeping earth is all it takes to banish dejection. Their primacy is recognized universally. Who does not love them? 'A snowdrop is a snowdrop is a snowdrop,' some would say. To the increasing number of galanthophiles this is heresy. There are more than 150 snowdrops listed and new varieties are being discovered all the time. Each is an individual.

The first and the best is *Galanthus nivalis*. Its simplicity and perfection of form are unsurpassed. There are bigger snowdrops. There are snowdrops with quirky markings or unusual forms, but none can outdo *G. nivalis*. At first one or two shoots peer outwards, inspecting the wintry scene like animals emerging gingerly from hibernation, sniffing the air. Each shoot lengthens gradually. The 'eye' of the stem eventually expands until the twin leaves which have held and protected the nascent bud agree it is time to part company and allow it to emerge. As the flower swells, and the stem lengthens, the papery sheath opens and the big, white drop is free to dangle and expand at the end of the hair-fine pedicel which joins it to its stem. No matter how fierce the weather, the flowers survive unscathed. The overhanging petals and their green-tipped underskirts bob and dance through gale and tempest, effortlessly protecting its inner workings. It is truly a feat of botanical engineering. Once the flower is pollinated, the ovary, to which the pedicel is joined, swells and the flower stem lengthens. This is the only stage in the snowdrop's career when it looks messy, but such untidiness is short-lived and essentially fruitful. The weight of the ovary brings it down to ground level where its casing eventually bursts or rots, exposing the seeds. When they germinate and make new bulbs, they do so far enough away from the parent plant to enable independent existence.

Snowdrops are seldom seen as isolated specimens. We always talk about them 'carpeting' a woodland floor, and the gradual whitening of a piece of dank earth which their emergence produces is magical. In common with so many Cinderella plants they are colonizers *par excellence*. In addition to the willingness of most to set seed, their bulbs sub-divide constantly so that clumps thicken and increase even without sex.

According to Christopher Lloyd, *G.* 'Atkinsii' never sets seed. I am not so sure, but however it does it there is no doubt that it spreads rapidly. This is a most welcome snowdrop. It arrives early, sometimes even before the wildings, and sometimes through snow. It is large, substantial but decidedly elegant with long, gently flared petals and broad, glaucous leaves. Although it will colonize quickly of its own volition, if you have a plan for it, you can dig it up as it fades, knock the soil from the bulbs and replant separately a few centimetres or inches apart and 10–15cm/4–6in deep.

Give each bulb a ration of good, humusy compost, preferably mixed with leaf mould. Vary distances between the bulbs to ensure a random, natural look. Within a short space of time you can create big drifts. This is the best procedure for replanting all snowdrops. Always plant them 'in the green',

Right

Snowdrops with golden ovaries and pedicels are rare and treasured. Discovered in a Cambridgeshire orchard by Mrs Sharman, Galanthus plicatus *'Wendy's Gold' has proved to be particularly vigorous and reliable. The purity and simplicity of its form are perfect.*

Right
Clockwise from top left
Galanthus nivalis
*'Viridapicis' is a striking
snowdrop, easily grown,
which has strong, solid
green markings on the
outer segments.* G.
plicatus *subsp.*
byzantinus *'Trym' is a
cult hybrid with outer
petals forming a Chinese
pagoda around the inner
petals.* G. *'John Gray' is a
classic, poised and
elegant, and one of the
biggest of all snowdrops.*
G. *'Jacquenetta' is neat
and very double – one of
the Greatorex doubles, all
of which are very similar
to the untrained eye!*

in active growth, with some evidence of roots and leaves. Never buy dry bulbs which are sometimes in such a state of dormancy that they may sleep, Rip van Winkle-like, for a hundred years.

To discover a plant at its peak when all around it is dormant and in many cases totally subterranean is an uplifting and encouraging experience. The wood anemone, *Anemone nemorosa*, is another true Cinderella, many of which are woodland plants with bulbs or tubers in which to store food until it is needed to produce new growth. *Anemone nemorosa* has small, skinny rhizomes which spread speedily through leaf litter just below the soil surface. Opportunists through and through, they colonize freely. Even the smallest piece of rhizome will rapidly make a new plant. As always, emulating nature is the simplest way to increase stock. Break small pieces of rhizome off the parent plant and replant with a little fresh compost or leaf mould 2–5cm/1–2in below the soil surface. If the weather is dry, water well and mulch with leaf mould or chipped bark. You can soon establish a thriving colony from one or two pots and in future years the process can be repeated to reproduce the kind of picture Mother Nature paints. This is best tackled during dormancy or just as the leaves are dying back.

Even when they are in full growth, a planting of wood anemones can disappear on a dull day. The flowers remain closed and hang their heads, protecting delicate and precious pollen from lashing rain. When the sun shines, stems straighten and the flowers are held aloft, fully open, revelling in the sun and announcing their presence to any pollinating insect which might chance by. As the sun moves across the clear spring sky, the flowers follow its course. The British native plant has white flowers, subtly shaded with lavender pink on their reverse. There are more than 40 recorded varieties of wood anemone. Some look very much alike, although there are subtle differences. Most are natural variants noticed by keen-eyed botanists and gardeners and introduced to civilized society on account of their unusual colour, the quality or size of their flower or an esoteric or occasionally quirky characteristic. Some are exceedingly beautiful, others excessively odd. None surpasses the simple beauty of the wild wood anemone.

Anemone nemorosa 'Robinsoniana' is a treasure. Like all wood anemones, it looks best *en masse*. Large, elegant buds of dove grey open to reveal chalices of purest azure, centred with a broad ring of quivering, golden stamens. Grown in contrast to yellow leaves – Bowles' golden grass (*Milium effusum* 'Aureum') or *Valeriana phu* 'Aurea' – the blue is made all the truer and the golden anthers are all the more noticeable.

Anemone nemorosa 'Robinsoniana' has real 'petal power' and, despite its lowly bearing, makes a striking impact in the spring garden. Some wood anemones have no petals at all. *Anemone nemorosa* 'Virescens' is a curiosity. Above mounds of typical finely cut foliage are heads of equally lacy, green bracts. As a filigree backcloth to more domineering spring players, such as hellebores and trilliums, it provides rich textural contrast in monochrome green.

Left

Anemone nemorosa
'Vestal' – as pure as she
sounds – is the belle of the
ball, with a profusion of
white petals turning each
flower into a perfect
powder puff, sitting on a
rosette of equally white
outer petals.

Above right

*The delicate flowers of a
semi-double* Anemonella
thalictroides, *a North
American woodlander.*

On its own it is easily overlooked. A similar variety, A. n. 'Bracteata Pleniflora', has the distinct advantage of a smattering of white petals within its bracts. Yet another oddity is A. n. 'Green Fingers' in which the arrangement is reversed. It has a cluster of green petals inside its white flowers.

The rue anemone, *Anemonella thalictroides*, is a heartachingly beautiful little plant with delicate flowers of white or pale pink. Native to the USA, it grows in woodland from New England to Florida and west to Kansas. Given the right conditions – shade, cool and humusy soil – anyone can grow both this plant and *Anemone nemorosa* anywhere. One of the major differences between the two is the leaves: whereas A. *nemorosa* has palmate, fingered leaves of dark green, *Anemonella thalictroides* has dainty leaves on wiry stems like those of a maidenhair fern or a Thalictrum. The other significant difference, especially for those who want to propagate their plants, is that A. *thalictroides* has tuberous roots all emanating from one crown which make it much more difficult to divide than its Old World cousin. It sets seed more prolifically than *Anemone nemorosa* though, and provided you watch your plants like a hawk, collecting the seed as soon as it ripens and sowing it fresh, stock can be increased. Both plants belong to the buttercup family, Ranunculaceae, the seed of which is greasy and can quickly deteriorate or become dormant. Surface sow it on soil-based compost, covering with

Right

Primula *'Lady Greer'*,
with rosettes of spoon-
shaped leaves and dainty
cream flowers, combines
beautifully with other
springtime plants that
relish partial shade and
humus-rich soil. It looks
particularly well with
the darker forms of
snakeshead fritillary.

a fine layer of grit or vermiculite. Water from below by standing your pot or tray in a shallow bowl and take it out and allow it to drain as soon as the surface of the grit is wet. Stand it in a cool place, out of direct sunlight. Seedlings need to be pricked out separately and allowed to grow on before being planted out.

Anemonella thalictroides also has a multitude of different forms. Those with semi-double flowers in white or pale pink are fairly widespread. They often come true from seed. Varieties with fully double flowers are precious collectors' items. Once you are hooked and provided you enjoy the thrill of the chase and have unlimited funds with which to pursue and acquire your quarry, you could build up an interesting collection, every one a gem. *Anemonella thalictroides* 'Oscar Schoaf' has pink flowers darkening towards its centre where the petals are most concentrated. It has row upon row of evenly placed petals. In fact the flower's formation is so mathematically perfect, it looks like an invention in an Elizabethan herbal where the drawing is based on a symmetrical shorthand rather than a description of nature. But nature it is, along with *A. t.* 'Alba Plena', a double white, and 'Green Hurricane' with lime green pom-poms. These double varieties are beloved of alpine show exhibitors who keep a close eye on them by growing them in pots.

The problem with all Cinderella plants, especially if you are keen and have limited space, is that you are liable to dig them up accidentally during their dormant season. It is too easy to plunge in the trowel or spade to plant a new acquisition whenever we see an 'empty space'. I have lost plant after plant of rue anemone through my own carelessness. It pays to mark them well at planting time.

Another plant which has also fallen foul of my over-zealous enthusiasm to plant something new is *Ranunculus aconitifolius* 'Flore Pleno'. Although it flowers later than the anemones, reaching the pinnacle of its accomplished performance just as spring thinks of giving way to summer, it too will disappear without trace during the hottest months. The single-flowered *R. aconitifolius* is a plant of alpine meadows. It loves deep, substantial soil and thrives in a damp situation. When happy, its airy, branching stems can reach 90cm/3ft, and as much across. It has handsome basal foliage from which its stems gradually extend, scattered with smaller leaves and a host of tiny, white buttercups. The whole impression is one of informality, almost abandon. 'Flore Pleno', the double-flowered cultivar, is a much more tailored and tidy sort of affair and is more compact, usually making 60cm/2ft at most. It is a plant to fall in love with. Each flower is a picture of perfection and a miracle of construction, with neatly overlapping petals, green at the centre and becoming pristine white, in layers, forming a complete ball.

The primrose, *Primula vulgaris*, is another irresistible stalwart. Its pale perfect petals with an egg-yolk centre on delicate stems the colour of pink skin nestling in rosettes of fresh green, crinkly leaves are a familiar sight in temperate regions throughout the world. Essentially a hedgerow or

edge-of-woodland plant, it loves damp, humus-laden soil where its fine, fibrous roots can reach out to find sustenance in the leaf litter. If we can replicate these conditions in our gardens, then the primrose and its many beautiful descendants will feel at home.

If the primrose were a new plant, discovered in some far-off land, we would all be fighting for it, anxious to be the first to put it in our gardens. But primulas have been in cultivation for centuries. Gerard's *Herbal* mentions several double forms already considered suitable garden flowers in the 16th century: the double white *P. vulgaris* 'Alba Plena', which is still a treasured plant today, and 'Lilacina Plena' or 'Quaker's Bonnet', one of the prettiest doubles. With a lax habit and a profusion of very refined lavender flowers, it is much more elegant than some of the modern doubles, which are increased in vast quantities now by micro-propagation.

Most of the doubles are sterile and division is the only way to make more. Gertrude Jekyll, who grew thousands of polyanthus in her coppiced hazel woods, described the best time to divide them as 'when the bloom wanes and is nearly overtopped by the leaves'. Varieties like *P.* 'Dawn Ansell', with a posy of pure white petals contained within a 'jack-in-the-green' ruff, are very desirable but most effective in groups. Several plants can be used to weave their way between dark hellebores or contribute to a green and white planting with *Leucojum aestivum* or *Pulmonaria* 'Sissinghurst White'.

Some primulas hibernate for the greater part of the year. *Primula sieboldii* is one of the many Asiatic primulas which spends summer, autumn and winter gathering strength for a dramatic spring display – broad, leafy clumps of bright, new green, bespangled with graceful flowers whose fragile beauty belies the plant's toughness. In the wild it grows in damp meadows and in the garden, as in nature, it will put up with competition from other plants which overtake later. It is an even-tempered plant, withstanding low winter temperatures and asking for little apart from moist soil and an occasional mulch which should guarantee its gentle spread.

Most Cinderella plants have devices for storing food and *Primula sieboldii* has small stolons or pips, each of which makes a separate flowering shoot. Other Asiatic primulas rely on seed to increase numbers. Many candelabra primulas, *P. japonica* and allied species, set masses of seed. Most love damp conditions and, although they will thrive in an open site, are at their best in wet places close to trees. Their flowering often coincides with the first beech leaves unscrolling their tender greenery. First they establish base camp with rosettes of crinkled leaves that get bigger day by day. Then up comes the flowering stem encircled by a carousel of buds. As these open, the stems lengthen and another circle of buds, tightly furled and often dusted with farina, emerges. The process continues until as many as eight or nine layers of flower grace the stem. By the time the last layer opens, the first may already have set seed. The plant has no mechanism for dispersing the seed to faraway places, but practises a saturation policy, producing thousands of seeds

Right
Erythronium
californicum *'White
Beauty'* has large,
creamy-white flowers,
each marked with a circle
of red as a pollen guide
for insects.

(one species is actually called *P. prolifera*), most of which will fall to the
ground close to the parent. Some germinate and a few survive to join the clan
as productive adults. As seed is set and summer heat increases, the rosettes
retract. By the end of summer there is no evidence of their existence, apart
from an occasional shrivelled stem and a host of fat resting buds. In true
Cinderella style they rest, awaiting the next spring.

The tubers of *Erythronium dens-canis* pull themselves down into pockets
of deep soil where they gradually build into dense clumps. The long, pointed
tubers, off-white and shiny, give rise to the plant's Latin and vernacular
names – dog's tooth violet. In fact erythroniums belong to the lily family and,
although diminutive compared to most of their bigger cousins, have huge
presence. They are all the more evident because of their earliness. First come
the beautifully mottled obovate leaves, followed in quick succession by long,
scrolled buds which rapidly unfurl when the warm spring sun hits them,
reflexing magically into pretty pink turks-cap flowers. At the fullest extent
of their growth they are no more than 10cm/4in high. This is the only Eurasian
species; the rest come from North America, though they are all such
irresistible plants that they have charmed gardeners throughout the
temperate world.

The American species, *Erythronium californicum* and *E. revolutum*, are
loftier beauties. *Erythronium californicum* is glorious. Its pink or white
flowers dangle gracefully from 30cm/1ft high stems, rising from thick, twin
leaves, richly marbled in bronze. It is widely distributed in woodland
throughout the Pacific northwest. It is a tolerant plant, adjusting itself to a
garden setting with ease. When happy it will seed around and, provided it is
left to its own devices, can colonize rapidly. A selection from it, *E.
californicum* 'White Beauty', is particularly fine with large, creamy-white
flowers each marked with a circle of red, a pollen guide for insects. The flower
stems are red too. The foliage is marbled, green on green, like looking into a
fast, clear stream when the light creates dappled patterns, darker areas
delineated by paler lines. Its vernacular name, trout lily, is very apt. Unlike
some of its wilder relatives it increases far too slowly, but is all the more
highly valued for its tardiness. Each spring its appearance is eagerly awaited
at Glebe Cottage and when the tips of the leaves peep through the dank soil
there is almost childish excitement. The re-emergence of all these springtime
Cinderellas is always hugely reassuring, a confirmation that the dark days of
winter are almost gone.

Yellow is the colour of a new spring and *Erythronium tuolumnense,* with
glossy, green leaves with undulating edges, and *E.* 'Pagoda', whose leaves are
sometimes slightly dappled, provide a wealth of rich yellow flowers on tall
(45cm/18in) stems. *E. tuolumnense* occurs often in damp places in the wild
and in the garden looks particularly well near water. Accompanied by the
stiff, new foliage of *Carex elata* 'Aurea' or the emerging swords of *Iris
pseudacorus* 'Variegata', the glowing yellow of its flowers is accentuated and

Preceding pages
*The dancing, prancing
turks-cap flowers of dog's
tooth violets,* Erythronium
dens-canis, *bring the
woodland floor to life.*
Opposite
Sanguinaria canadensis
f. multiplex *'Plena', the
double form of bloodroot,
is a woodland wonder.*

their nodding grace emphasized in contrast to the sharp uprights. Even when its home has been flooded during the winter, it comes through with consummate ease, energetically blooming as though it had relished the extra soak. With changing weather patterns this is a plant which may adapt easily to increasingly flooded gardens.

Blood root, *Sanguinaria canadensis,* is a woodland wonder from eastern North America which copes well with drier conditions. It is a one-off, the only *Sanguinaria* within the family Papaveraceae. Its emerging leaves closely resemble those of *Macleaya cordata,* the plume poppy, in texture and form if not in size. The whole plant, including the thick, spreading rootstock which bleeds red sap when damaged, is succulent and fleshy. Each emerging flower bud is wrapped tightly in one scalloped leaf which unfurls as the flower stem pushes up its fragile flower. The simple, pure white flowers are fleeting, almost ghostly in their transparence, seldom lasting more than a day or two – a mere nuance of a flower.

Less graceful but much longer-lasting, the double form, *Sanguinaria canadensis* f. *multiplex,* is more often cultivated and probably more garden-worthy. Its chunky, globose flowers are laden generously with pristine petals, in telling contrast to the puckered grey of its protecting leaf. Once seen, never forgotten, this is an ooh-aah, can't-live-without-it plant. Its preference is for leafy, acid soil but even when conditions seem perfect it sometimes disappears, much to its owner's chagrin. Addicts, however, never give up. There are gardeners who have tried as many as seven or eight times to establish this temperamental beauty despite increasingly large holes in their bank balances as well as their shady borders.

Jeffersonia diphylla is of the same ilk, transient and fleeting, but is easier to satisfy. It belongs to a different family, the Berberidaceae. It too comes from eastern North America but grows on leafy limestone soils. Its small, white flowers are almost hidden by the twin leaves which grow up past the flowers on 20cm/8in stems. As they emerge they clasp each other, palm to palm like praying hands, but when they reach their zenith they open and separate, looking for all the world like emerald butterflies.

Jeffersonia dubia is a precious plant. Although it is more often seen on the show benches of alpine gardening societies, it is perfectly happy in the garden, but again prone to danger from invading trowels during its long sleep. *Jeffersonia dubia* 'Alba' is the white form, but it usually has blue flowers. Blue hardly describes them. They are pale azure, the colour concentrated in the buds and becoming more transparent and celestial as the flowers open. The contrast with the small, epimedium-like leaves, which are dark and purple-tinged as they emerge, makes the flowers seem all the paler. This species hails from Manchuria and is also found in eastern Russia and South Korea.

Podophyllum are typical of the plants that have to accomplish their whole cycle of flowering and setting seed before the clock strikes twelve. By the time the fruit is ripe the leaves and stems have practically disintegrated, their

Preceding pages
*Side by side, the flowers
of* Jeffersonia dubia *and*
Podophyllum hexandrum
*reveal the family
resemblance, although
they are borne quite
differently. The delicate
chalices of the jeffersonia
push themselves above the
horizontal leaves. In*
Podophyllum hexandrum
*the flower sits on the
bridge between the leaves
and later will become
a fat, red berry.*
Opposite
Each tessellated bell of
Fritillaria meleagris *looks
hand-painted. Here
purple snakeshead
fritillaries mingle with
an albino form.*

goodness absorbed back into the fleshy rootstock which will rest until next spring when the furled umbrella tips will emerge once again. *Podophyllum hexandrum* is a cousin of *Jeffersonia*. It is a bold plant whose twin, palmate leaves are splashed with dark purple as they emerge and assume their typical horizontal stance at the summit of the 30cm/1ft high stems. The family resemblance to *Jeffersonia* is hard to spot until the small, pink or white flowers emerge. Their dainty form and frail texture are similar, although borne quite differently, riding the bridge between the leaves. After the petals fall, the leaf stem continues to grow and the flower's small ovary swells. When mature it becomes a large, red fruit. Some say it is edible, although Christopher Lloyd declares it poisonous. Since I trust his Epicurean judgement implicitly I am not going to try it.

Other *Podophyllum* species have been introduced to the West from Asia, many of which have strikingly patterned foliage. On a trip to the Pacific northwest I was privileged to see new seedlings of *P. difforme* grown from seed collected by Dan Hinkley and Darrell Probst. Every one was different and every one highly desirable. The texture of some is sumptuous, one of the most velvety being *P. delavayi*.

Fritillaria meleagris, the snakeshead fritillary, likes nothing better than the hurly-burly of the open garden. With luck it will seed itself around. A plant of water-meadows, in its wild habitat the snakeshead fritillary grows cheek by jowl with grasses and meadow flowers that enjoy the same conditions – meadow buttercups, lady's smock, ragged robin and greater burnet. The regime of old water-meadows suited it perfectly. During winter and early spring low-lying land beside rivers would be deliberately flooded to enrich the soil. In spring, as the water subsided, perennial plants and grasses would grow vigorously. Later in the year the field would be cut for hay for winter cattle fodder. By this time most of the plants, including snakeshead fritillary, would have set and distributed seed to further enrich and renew the meadow. In spring grey-green stems support fabulously tessellated, pendulous bells, in every shade of purple and white, barely 30cm/1ft high. They are hardly recognizable later. The stems grow to 60–90cm/2–3ft, topped with upright seed capsules, the whole thing dry and corn-coloured. The fat seed capsules split into sections from the top, exposing layers of neatly stacked, wafer-thin seeds which are blown hither and thither on windy days.

Many members of the lily family disperse their seed in this way and will sow themselves randomly wherever they land. It is during midsummer that fritillaries disperse their seed after which they sleep through summer, autumn and winter until once again spring summons them into growth.

No matter that Cinderella plants bow out early and spend most of the year underground – however short their moment of glory, it is earth-shattering.

2.

Bread-and-butter plants

Left

Late-summer colour in my garden with stalwart Rudbeckia fulgida *var.* deamii *and* Achillea *'Terracotta', spiky sea holly,* Eryngium x zabelii *'Violetta' and vivid yellow and red crocosmia for added drama.*

These are the stalwarts, the good-natured and easy-to-please herbaceous plants without whom our beds and borders would descend into a sea of anarchy and chaos. By contrast with the fleeting Cinderellas, they make a contribution to the overall picture for months. The focus may be on one group at a particular time, but as growth and season change the spotlight shifts to other associations. Many have robust foliage and are floriferous over a long period. Some have attractive seed heads, while others will flower again if they are deadheaded or cut back. Few need staking and most will grow steadily outwards, demanding only to be lifted and divided every few years to keep them on the go. Sounds too sensible and predictable? Not a bit of it. These plants combine two of the most desirable qualities we gardeners seek: staying power and pulling power.

SOME OF THE MOST STRAIGHTFORWARD yet vivacious funsters are daisies, members of the family Asteraceae, long known as Compositae. They have simple flowers and strong stems and are not attractive exclusively to humankind. Many are an important source of nectar to pollinating insects, and seed-eating birds gorge on the feast they supply deep into the winter, provided autumn tidying-up has not been too thorough. Most are midsummer plants whose flowering continues into the autumn, although many of the smaller-flowered asters or Michaelmas daisies do not start until the days begin to shorten. They share their glory with richly coloured crocosmias, golden grasses and other late daisies.

The simple perfection of the flowers of *Aster x frikartii* 'Mönch' is available for months, making it one of the most desirable plants in the garden. It is a blue daisy with a golden, spiralling centre. On first opening, this centre or disc is touched with green. In all daisies the disc is a composite of tiny flowers and the petals are no more than a lure to interest pollinating insects and guide them towards the centre of the action. In 'Mönch' these petals are long and refined and beautifully blue. The blue of all asters has red in it rather than yellow, pushing their colour towards lilac. 'Mönch' is as blue as they get. It was one of three hybrids between *A. amellus* and *A. thomsonii* bred in 1920 by Herr Frikart in Switzerland. He named his selections after three famous Swiss mountains, Eiger, Mönch and Jungfrau. Although the other two are worthy plants, 'Mönch' is head and shoulders above them. It has balance both within the flower and between the flowers and the structure of the whole plant. It needs no staking and although it is always good practice to deadhead daisies, if it is not done flowering will not be impaired.

Many of the over-hybridized *Aster novi-belgii* varieties are disappointing. Their habit is awkward and dumpy and they are almost always smitten with mildew, sometimes to the extent that they appear to have white foliage. If, like me, you garden organically, they are not worth growing. In complete contrast are several species asters, selections from them and some of their simple, first-generation hybrids, which retain the wild beauty of their parents and are trouble-free. They look as though they belong – natural and artless – in laid-back plantings and can also be used in sophisticated and sometimes amusing ways.

At Great Dixter in Sussex, Christopher Lloyd hedged an area reserved for stock plants with *Aster lateriflorus* 'Horizontalis' where its outstretched branches joined hands to provide an unusual edging. This aster may not be spectacular, but it oozes personality. Early in the season, from a rosette of glossy leaves, it sends up vertical stems which, as they reach their full height, in turn send out stiff branches at right angles. In due course these are covered with small, beetroot-dark leaves and eventually in tiny, pale daisies with maroon centres. Long after the onset of winter, the stiff stems, with leaves and seed heads still adhering to them, continue to lend structure and colour, even if by now it is a subtle, monochrome biscuit.

Right
Aster x frikartii *'Mönch'*
is a plant to sing songs
about or turn cartwheels
for or in whose honour to
light a firework display.
Its perfect daisies disport
themselves for months,
adding a touch of class
wherever they appear.

Aster divaricatus is another daisy valued for its structure, albeit of a completely different nature. It makes clumps of glossy, rich green leaves from which rise wiry, branching, black stems producing myriad tiny, white stars. The stems arch over gracefully until, just as it seems its opening flowers will weigh them down, the stems 'set' and stay – perfectly poised to display the starry flowers to best advantage. This aster does not need full sun to thrive. Gertrude Jekyll, who called it *A. corymbosus*, recommended it for growing over the unsightly remains of plants past their best – dog-eared bergenias or *passé* poppies.

There are asters for everywhere and everyone. I want them all and find it difficult to choose, but one which I could not live without is *Aster* 'Little Carlow' (*cordifolius* hybrid). I first saw it at Powis Castle near Welshpool, Powys. Its big clouds of pure and brilliant blue were visible from a distance, hovering over the steep terraces. Its impact is just as spellbinding at close quarters. Large corymbs of flat, solid blue, individual daisies with crisp, crimson centres and neat petals top tall stems. Even on a windy site the strong stems remain upright without staking. 'Little Carlow' is resilient in every way, its dark, elegant leaves unblemished by disease, and it seems to thrive and increase in even the coldest gardens. In good, fertile soil it will reach 1.2m/4ft. The majority of this growth is not made until the back end of the summer, but before then its healthy basal foliage gives glossy green infill among earlier-flowering subjects, summer cranesbills and sea hollies. It seems happy to bide its time, confident in the knowledge of forthcoming glory. Incapable of clashing or looking out of place, this aster turns aggressive competitors into perfect partners and adds quality to the most mundane planting. It is a worthy companion for *Rudbeckia*.

The glorious prairie daisies are the essence of reliability but with such exuberant charm that we would grow them even if they were to fold after only one season. In fact, clumps go on for years. All perennial rudbeckias are yellow. Some gardeners are snooty about yellow. I used to be one of them. Even before I started gardening I was off yellow. As a fine-art student I arbitrarily decided to give yellow a miss for a whole year until I was told, rather pointedly, that yellow was the colour of spirituality. By this argument *Rudbeckia fulgida* var. *deamii* must be one of the most spiritual of plants. Its flowers are certainly among the most yellow of yellows. Large, golden discs, their colour made all the more intense by black, velvety centres, open in huge abundance during early autumn and continue in succession until its end. In some years they go on glowing into the first murky days of winter and the black central cones persist long after that, making bobbly thickets among sere grasses.

Flowering at its usual time, a few clumps or even one large plant of *Rudbeckia fulgida* var. *deamii* can create a feeling of ease, as though summer would last indefinitely. It is an archetypal 'Indian summer' plant. But before the yellowness gets going there is a green lull. Towards the end of summer

Right

The raised cones of
Echinacea purpurea, *the
purple coneflower, are full
of nectar for butterflies
and other pollinators.
Later the seed heads
provide food for hungry
birds and are a bonus
in the garden, adding
winter interest among
tall grasses.*

each bushy plant has finished its construction phase. Branches and stems pause, buds swell imperceptibly. As the pointed, green calyces open into green stars, the back of the petals, slender and green, are revealed. Slowly they broaden and stretch until they lie on the horizontal beds the calyx has provided. At this stage gardeners inspect their plants daily, anxiously anticipating the first flash of yellow. Once it starts, given even a modicum of sunshine, flower follows glorious flower until the whole plant glows gold. At the height of its glory its flower power is so over-powering that the green leaves are almost imperceptible.

Every plant family has its 'choice' variety. *Rudbeckia maxima* is the one here. It is an elegant plant with a slightly haughty air, probably created by its flowers whose tall, black central cones launch themselves upwards as its long petals droop downwards disdainfully. Its foliage is unique among that of coneflowers, consisting of a rosette of long, paddle-shaped, glaucous leaves, each with an elongated stem. Because it is late into flower it sometimes gets tucked at the back of a border but deserves a front seat where its beautiful, blue-grey foliage can be appreciated. The flower stems are almost bare and easy to see through and the beauty of its flowers can be appreciated when viewed at close quarters.

Very closely related to *Rudbeckia* is the purple coneflower, *Echinacea purpurea*. Another member of the stalwart plants' first team, it is popular in 'prairie planting' schemes, and equally renowned among those who put their faith in alternative medicine and homeopathic remedies. In the garden its robust, pinky-purple daisies inspire a feeling of well-being, especially when their anthers appear, lighting up the bronze central cones with fiery orange. In some plants the petals are almost horizontal, in others gently drooping. Most of the plants offered for sale are seed-raised and this accounts for the wide variations in both the colour and form of the flowers. Either choose your plant in flower or try it from seed and select your own seedlings. There are several named forms available of deeper colour, larger flower size or shorter habit. To live up to their pedigree they must be vegetatively propagated either by physical division or micro-propagation. Some of them miss the point. The characteristic cone is flattened and diminished. It always seems a pity when hybridization loses an intrinsic quality of the plant it is purporting to 'improve'.

Dividing *Echinacea purpurea* is not as easy a job as splitting rudbeckias. The plants tend to have a woody centre and it is difficult to get purchase either with fingers or forks to break up the crowns into viable pieces. On my heavy clay *E. purpurea* is not long-lived, probably needing better drainage than I can supply, but if you are gardening on a lighter, fertile soil it should last for years. White varieties are popular, especially among gardeners of the 'subtle persuasion'. Their white is not the bright white of shasta daisies but a much more understated greenish white, a sort of 'looking-at-white-through-mist-or-seawater' kind of white. This is much easier to use in a

mixed planting than brash white and of course these flowers always have the added attraction of the typical, orange-lit cones which persist long after the petals fade.

The buds of all *Echinacea* are attractive. They are big and solid, packed with promise and excitement as the central boss gradually rises from the crunchy calyx and the embryonic petals push inexorably outwards. Several other North American daisies exhibit unusual raised centres. Those of *Helenium* are almost spherical, characteristically velvety dark brown or golden yellow. They are perfectly complemented by soft, undulating petals which either hang down or stick out vertically, surrounding the central boss like a ballet dancer's tutu. No white or pale pink for them, though. *Helenium* are gay and jolly flowers, bright chrome yellow, deep crimson and bronze, or combinations of any or all of these. They flower prolifically and they make their mark not by great subtlety but by straightforward flower power. Their flowers are blatant and bouncy.

Helenium 'Moerheim Beauty' is an old variety which can still give modern hybrids a run for their money. Cut back hard after its summer flowering, it will produce another display of its velvet-bronze flowers with their rich brown, furry doorknob middles. There are few other species which produce so wide a range of size and scale. If you need a helenium 1.5m/5ft tall to fill the breach among tall *Monarda, Miscanthus, Verbena bonariensis* and like-minded subjects in a 'prairie planting', then *Helenium* 'Summer Circle' makes a broad, branching plant full of yellow flowers late in the season. *Helenium*, along with most of these North American daisies, are plants of the disappeared prairies.

Hay meadows are the European equivalent and, like the prairies, have been sacrificed to modern mono-culture. The rich mixture of grasses and perennial flowers which they contained has fled to the boundaries of their ancient territory, ousted by rye grass and destroyed by hormone weed-killers. Hedgerows and road verges have become their sanctuary. Our gardens, too, can offer a safe haven. Indeed, many of the beautiful flowers which formerly jostled amongst vernal grasses and sweet herbs have long been cultivated in gardens. *Geranium pratense* is a typical example. In fact it is so at home in my garden, self-seeding prolifically, that unless I am assiduous about decapitation as soon as the petals have fallen, and equally brutal about taking out unwanted youngsters who have already established a foothold, we are overrun with meadow cranesbill. But some summers, when I have missed my mission in the previous year, I am glad I did. The garden is a great sea of colour, from white and palest grey, through pale pink, to every imaginable shade of blue. This rich variety has all come miraculously from one original blue-flowered plant.

There are many other deserving plants which need their allotted place, and sooner or later restrictions have to be imposed. There are two double varieties of *Geranium pratense* which pose no threat of invasion. As with most double flowers, they have no ovaries and are incapable of producing seed – sad for them, but a boon for gardeners. *Geranium pratense* 'Plenum Caeruleum' starts its long display in early summer, sending out stem after branching stem of warm blue flowers touched with lilac. It is just as devil-may-care in effect as many of its single sisters, but never develops their typical 'cranesbill' seed heads. Its flowers are loosely double whereas the flowers of *G. p.* 'Plenum Violaceum' make perfectly symmetrical rosettes. Each flower forms a separate posy and each stem produces great bunches of flowers, until the plant looks like one enormous bouquet. Deadhead when the first flowers begin to look shabby and the next batch, already budding up, will be as good as the first. In any case, flowers will be produced late into the summer and early autumn. The plants have strong stems and need no staking, although they are always happiest with a few friends for mutual support. Their soft colours blend so easily with those of neighbouring plants that it would be difficult to make a jarring statement with any meadow cranesbill. The big, lemon daisies of *Anthemis tinctoria* 'Wargrave Variety' or *A. t.* 'E.C. Buxton' make a delicious accompaniment.

Geranium psilostemon is magnificent and its large, black-centred, magenta flowers above bold, palmate foliage could not be more assertive. This is a true bread-and-butter plant, exhibiting all the qualities of the *joie-de-vivre* club. Early in spring, the new, crimson shoots pushing through the bare earth are as exciting as the launch of the first snowdrop spears. The handsome leaves, which form big clumps 90cm/3ft wide and as much high, are glossy green throughout the season and often take on orange and red tints during autumn. It is one of those plants which grows in stature year by year, provided it is supplied with an occasional hearty mulch of rotted muck. When it shows signs of dwindling, it is easy to rejuvenate by dividing and replanting in soil mixed with good compost and a sprinkling of organic fertilizer. Ensure that the roots are evenly spread out and that the planting mixture is gently but firmly packed around them so that no air pockets remain.

Geranium psilostemon is such a good all-rounder, it is difficult not to over-use it. Its striking flowers are borne in abundance from early summer through to the time its leaves turn to fiery orange. One of its children, *G.* 'Ann Folkard', combines the same scintillating, black-centred, magenta flowers with warm yellow foliage on sprawling growth which can reach as much as 1.2–1.5m/4–5ft in each direction. One plant can create high drama, especially if its effect is intensified by marrying it with the right partner.

Several big spurges which, through their strong and straightforward characters, belong with these *joie-de-vivre* plants, have bracts of a similar colour, though of completely different form, to those of the geranium. The strong, upright stems supporting the statuesque, bracted heads are lent another dimension when swathed in the butter-yellow foliage of the geranium. As the flowers open yet another act unfolds. In well-drained soils *Euphorbia characias*, especially its varieties with the most vivid yellow bracts,

in situ with sand added to the planting hole. Water well until they are established. Plants will benefit from a mulch of good compost or old manure after being cut back. Delay this as long as possible since thistle seeds are a delicacy to finches. Butterflies, bees and hoverflies will visit thistle flowers constantly as they provide a rich source of nectar.

Cirsium rivulare 'Atropurpureum' heads the field as the most desirable of all thistles. It is a tall, branching plant, each stem terminating in several rich-crimson flowers. The skinny, upright petals are close-packed and of even length, giving the impression of having been sliced horizontally to ensure symmetry. In farming folklore thistles are associated with good ground and their presence is supposed to indicate fertile land. When planting, prepare the ground well, incorporating plenty of humus-rich material – good, homemade compost is best.

Some thistles are as exciting in seed as they are in full flower. Not so *Cirsium rivulare* 'Atropurpureum'. Its soft seed heads tend to break up and look dishevelled, especially after rain. It puts on its first show in early summer and, as the flowers finish, it is best to trim back each side shoot to the main stem. This severe deadheading promotes new flowers and if they in their turn are cut back, the flowering season can be extended until the first frosts. When the last flowers fade, chop the whole stem to ground level. While you are tidying, it is worth giving the leaves a trim too. This is a first-rate thistle with second-rate foliage.

It is the foliage of some thistles that is their *raison d'être* and, while the cardoon (*Cynara cardunculus*) and the artichoke (*C. scolymus*) were originally cultivated to be eaten, their worth as long-lived and exuberant

Left
*The huge, thistly flowers
of the cardoon,* Cynara
cardunculus, *create a
crescendo at the end of
summer, standing high
above majestic, deeply cut,
silver foliage.*

members of the bread-and-butter group cannot be over-emphasized. They may have big, crunchy calyces and delightful heads of glistening purple late in the season, but it is the great, jagged, grey leaves that are their most important contribution, adding dramatic high spots to herbaceous plantings throughout the growing season. Both make excellent specimen plants in gravel, towering over mats of thyme or other Mediterranean carpeting plants.

Thistles are not a bit prickly when it comes to mingling with other plants. They are good mixers, an important characteristic for plants in this group. At the same time their conspicuous foliage and impressive flowers ensure they never get lost in the crowd. The architectural structure of the bigger thistles can be enhanced by mixing them with the great, nebulous heads of *Campanula lactiflora*. The milky bellflower is aptly named. Although it may be blue or white, the blue-flowered forms always have quantities of white mixed in with their blue, and the white of the white forms is always tinged with blue.

An established plant of *Campanula lactiflora* can make as many as twenty or more symmetrically arranged stems over a summer. From a handsome, basal rosette of long leaves, these stand up strongly, growing as high as 1.2m/4ft. Each supports a branching, terminal head of scores of small bellflowers with their edges turned out. When the initial flowers have faded, a swift decapitation allows subsidiary flowers on side shoots to open fully and prolong the performance. These secondary flowers cannot recreate the same billowing, cloudy effect as the first, but they are useful for filling in among late flowers and grasses.

Summer borders are places where plants need to get on well – no room for prima donnas here – and bellflowers are great team players. One of the most persistent in my garden is *Campanula persicifolia*. It seems mean-spirited to begin a list of its virtues by talking about its longevity, since it is one of the most beautiful and poetic of summer garden flowers. It forms evergreen rosettes of narrow, pointed leaves, hence its specific epithet and its common name, the peach-leaved bellflower. But however satisfactory these evergreen clumps may be, it is not for its leaves that we grow it. From midsummer onwards straight stems shoot up vertically from the low, carpeting foliage until, at about 60cm/2ft, they stop to concentrate on opening their fat buds. The species plant has simple, single bells in blue or white. It seeds prolifically and seedlings may vary in flower colour and stature and occasionally in form.

Over hundreds of years variants of *Campanula persicifolia* have been noticed and selected by observant gardeners and growers and there is a rich store of varieties from which today's gardeners can choose. Some have double flowers, others cup-in-saucer or even cup-in-cup. There are exquisitely coloured forms like 'Chettle Charm' (sometimes called 'George Chiswell' or 'Blue Edge'), in which the pure white flowers are gradually and very subtly imbued with blue as though each bell had been wetted and dipped momentarily in blue ink. The best, white, cup-in-saucer variety (not pure

Right
Campanula 'Sarastro' is
one of many east–west
crosses within the
bellflower family. The
purple of its waxy, tubular
flowers is particularly
rich, and especially so in
the pleated buds.

white; there is a helping of light green mixed in with the white) is 'Hampstead White'. 'Boule de Neige' is a white double with tight, full rosettes. Blue cup-in-cup is my favourite. It has great substance, the double layer of petals serving not only to support individual blooms which look out at you from the stem, but also to help each flower last longer. Double forms are sterile, cannot set seed and therefore their flowers stay longer on the plant and their flowering season is extended. 'Bennett's Blue' is a beauty, with powdery-blue, intensely double flowers.

Campanula latifolia is a native of the British Isles, frequenting scrubby areas on woodland margins or river banks. In a garden, without competition from coarse grasses and other rampant wild plants, it can be a strong, structural element. From a handsome, basal rosette of long leaves, several stems symmetrically arranged stand up firmly, growing as high as 1.2m/4ft. The buds are shiny and pointed, upward-facing, but as they open the waxy bells hang down, eventually reflexing gently at the mouth to enable bees to access their nectar and spread their pollen. Both blue and white forms are classically elegant plants but neither can hold a torch to *C. latifolia* 'Gloaming' with bells of silvery-grey defined by a centre of rich, dark purple.

Campanula latifolia is the probable parent of two of the most desirable bellflower hybrids. The parentage of *C.* 'Burghaltii' is unconfirmed, but almost certainly it is a cross between *C. latifolia* and *C. punctata* from Asia. This happy east–west union has resulted in a refined, graceful child with heart-shaped leaves, deep-purple, shiny buds and palest grey, waxy flowers. It is a 'must-have' plant. Should you grow it for a few years then lose it, you will pine until you find a replacement.

Campanula takesimana 'Elizabeth' is named for Elizabeth Strangman and was found on her Washfield Nursery in Kent, now sadly closed. Both she and her nursery have enriched our gardening vocabulary by contributing a wealth of good plants. 'Elizabeth' is an immensely valuable plant, spreading freely with running white roots and flowering exuberantly. Its bells are long and pendulous, of deep rosy-red marked with rich crimson. The flower stems are about 45cm/18in high, perhaps a little taller when grown in shade which it tolerates well.

Many campanulas can thrive in shade and because of their late flowering are particularly useful to fill the gaps in places left bare by the temporary disappearance of the spring woodlanders. Most of these border bellflowers are easily grown in almost any soil which is not waterlogged. Many European varieties make mats of fibrous root and both they and their Asiatic cousins with superficial running roots benefit from a mulch of bark or compost which helps retain moisture. Flowers of herbaceous varieties will be bigger and better with a helping of rotted dung applied during the winter and evergreen varieties like *C. persicifolia* and *C. latiloba* benefit from a dilute liquid feed applied after flowering. Organic, seaweed-based products work best.

All species campanulas can be grown from seed. If you are collecting your own, be aware that campanulas disperse their seed through small holes which

such as *E. c.* subsp. *wulfenii* 'Lambrook Gold' and 'John Tomlinson', fits the bill perfectly. In wetter conditions *E. palustris* or *E. schillingii*, a big, bold Asiatic spurge, could play host to the golden-leaved geranium.

Obsessively tidy gardeners complain about the wayward ramblings of *Geranium* 'Ann Folkard', but those who admire plants with a bit of spirit welcome her and find a multitude of situations where her independent nature can serve their purpose. This is an excellent subject for tumbling over walls or scrambling through dull foliage. The plant's relationship to its mother can be plainly seen in the flowers. Its scrambling habit is inherited from the other parent, *G. procurrens*, a wandering cranesbill from the foothills of the Himalayas.

Geranium 'Salome' is a cross between *G. procurrens* and *G. lambertii*, with all the grace of the second and none of the rapacity of the first. It is a very desirable cranesbill with rounded, uplifted, lilac flowers with darker veining and, as its name implies, dark and mysterious eyes. It is steadfast enough to take its place among the stalwart plants but it is difficult to increase. In common with *G. lambertii* and *G.* 'Ann Folkard', its growth dies back to the centre in winter. The best way to make more is with basal cuttings – short pieces taken from the crown of the plant as growth starts in spring. Cut cleanly below the lowest leaf node, remove the bottom leaves with a sharp knife and push these cuttings around the edge of a pot or seed tray in coarse, gritty compost. They root most readily when bottom heat is provided. The parent plant will soon make up for the theft of its bottom shoots.

There are so many good geraniums which could be included here. Some I exclude because of their relatively short flowering season, some are plants for very specific situations – hot sun or woodland shade – but for most it is just a question of having to choose. We will meet a few of the more select later on and a few of the really pushy individuals are bound to insinuate themselves somewhere.

Once upon a time respectable gardeners would not have given thistles garden space, but now they are 'must-have' plants, given pride of place in many a trendy garden design. At a princely 1.8m/6ft, with large, white spheres held on strong, white stems, *Echinops tournefortii* 'Albus' makes a stately presence. More compact but still of goodly size (up to 1.2m/4ft), the globe thistle, *E. ritro* subsp. *ruthenicus*, is a border stalwart – as its regular appearance in herbaceous borders far and wide attests. It is one of the few thistles to be admitted to polite (garden) society. Individual plants have a long life span, reliably producing their blue, drumstick flowers throughout the summer. Even before the slender, individual flowers open, the spherical heads make an impact, silvery at first and gradually changing to blue as circle after circle of flowers opens. These are nectar-rich but their long corolla tubes make the feast most easily available to moths with their elongated proboscis. Like artichokes and cardoons, echinops can be increased by detaching side shoots with a sharp knife at their base in April and planting

Left

In cultivation for centuries, Campanula persicifolia *has yielded all manner of variations, none more ravishing than* C. persicifolia *'Bennett's Blue' with powdery-blue, intensely double flowers.*

open at the back of the seed capsule. If you wait for the pods to open at the front you may miss the seed! Named hybrid campanulas may be sterile or, when they do set seed, may not come true. For instance, seed from *Campanula lactiflora* 'Loddon Anna', a delightful, lilac-flowered form, will yield seedlings with blue or white flowers. In both cases increase of the true plant is possible only by division or, more successfully, from basal cuttings.

The big, lemon discs of *Cephalaria gigantea*, a giant scabious from Siberia, are a perfect complement to the tall, fluffed-up heads of *Campanula lactiflora* 'Loddon Anna'. There is a hint of the bellflower's grey-lilac within the centre of the scabious flowers. It would never be noticed in the general run of things, but it is such details which give *frisson* to plant associations. This magnificent plant will reach 1.8m/6ft by early summer when it opens the first of its fat buds. Its later flowers are even more useful – their fresh, pale primrose is such an invigorating colour and so useful to splash about in the border amongst complacent blues and pinks that might otherwise fall asleep.

Scabiosa columbaria var. *ochroleuca* provides yet more piquancy with knee-high bushes of neat, glaucous rosettes below branching stems, bobbing with little lemon pom-poms. Its counterpart in deep alizarin crimson is *Knautia macedonica*, one of the most useful of all herbaceous plants, in flower from late spring through to the frosts and often beyond. It produces an abundance of flowers which obligingly shed their petals to reveal equally charming, spherical seed heads. The plants never need deadheading. In this case setting seed does not impair flower production. Because it never knows when to stop, it can become slightly chaotic and it is just as well to shear back all the top-growth mid-season. This does not mean forgoing too many flowers. Before you know it, buds will appear and flowering will be back to normal within a few weeks. If a liquid, organic, high-potash feed is administered, the new flowers will be bigger and better than ever.

All flowers of the scabious group have an outer circle of showy petals surrounding the centre of fertile florets where all the real business goes on. Often the anthers are a contrasting colour to the florets. In some of the very darkest forms they are white, which makes a startling combination. The dark varieties of *Scabiosa atropurpurea* have almost-black flowers lit with white anthers. Despite preaching a philosophy of 'right plant right place', I have ignored my own advice on several occasions and tried to grow the gorgeous large-flowered *S. caucasica*. It loves lime and sharp drainage, so my heavy, slightly acid soil is anathema. The small-flowered scabious, though, seem to enjoy life with me. Often their flowers are likened to pin cushions and this analogy is also made with the flowers of *Astrantia*, another border stalwart.

Astrantia major is a European native, a plant of damp meadows and the fringes of woods, with cultural requirements the opposite of my much-lamented *Scabiosa caucasica*. It loves substantial soil, the heavier the better, and is easy about alkalinity. During prolonged dry spells, especially when it has seeded itself into paths, as is its wont, and has no access to rich, deep

Above left
Astrantia major *subsp.*
involucrata *'Shaggy'*
became famous in the
garden and writings of
Margery Fish. In common
with many of the plants
she singled out, it is
exceptional, with long
bracts and green tips.
Right
Scabiosa atropurpurea
'Chat Noir', a seed strain
of sweet scabious, brings
dark excitement to the
garden border.

soil, it suffers badly. Astrantias have a multitude of vernacular names alluding to the unusual form of their flowers, as in Hattie's pin cushion, or to their equally unusual colour. 'Melancholy gentleman' perfectly sums up the quiet, unobtrusive greenish white of the bracted flowers.

Given what it likes, *Astrantia* is one of the most reliable and useful of garden plants. It flowers non-stop from late spring to late autumn. The only difficulty encountered in its cultivation is when to chop off the first flowers. Each head is composed of a circle of bracteoles, which look at first sight like petals, containing a multitude of tiny flowers – the pins in the pin cushion – forming a large umbel at the top of 60cm/2ft stems. These rise from a big, healthy clump of dark green, palmate leaves with toothed edges. In *A. major* 'Sunningdale Variegated', the leaves are heavily margined with cream when they emerge, making bold splashes of light and continuing to give extra value until midsummer. If the foliage is sheared back later in the season, the new leaves will be almost as startling as the first. Planting bronze-leaved subjects alongside this variegated astrantia maximizes the brilliance of the foliage. An entirely different texture can be used too – with the fluffy froth of bronze fennel or the fern-like foliage of *Anthriscus sylvestris* 'Raven's Wing' the contrast is even more emphatic.

Dark crimson astrantia have become *de rigueur* in any self-respecting herbaceous planting. The demand for varieties like *Astrantia major* 'Hadspen Blood' and 'Ruby Wedding' is such that micro-propagation is used to keep up the supply. I prefer to grow new plants from seed. There are several good

Preceding pages
*Deep crimson
masterworts are all the
rage.* Astrantia major
*'Gill Richardson' is an
especially striking
selection. Astrantias
always give extra value,
their bracts lasting
for months.*
Opposite
*Achillea 'Terracotta'
contributes vibrant colour
that gradually softens to
biscuit shades.*

seed strains available, but although astrantia seeds itself around in the garden with abandon, it is notoriously difficult to grow deliberately from seed, especially when it is not absolutely fresh. This is best guaranteed by collecting your own seed. All you need to produce dark-flowered seedlings are one or two good crimson-flowered parents. Each of the tiny flowers will set a seed, so one plant may produce hundreds. Take the seed just as it is ready to fall and surface sow it on loam-based seed compost, allowing enough room between seeds for each to grow. Cover with grit and leave the trays or pots outside. If you can give them bottom heat in a propagator or from soil-warming cables, it is worth trying this with a few pots. If the seed has not become dormant, it may germinate immediately. If it does not germinate within a few weeks, move the trays outside with the rest. A few cold nights should induce the seed to germinate. After this, take some of them under cover, to the greenhouse bench or a light windowsill, and hopefully little cotyledon leaves will soon emerge, followed swiftly by the first true leaves. If this works, bring in the rest. Grow the seedlings on, pricking out individually into module trays or small separate pots. These can either be potted on or, when big enough to survive the great outdoors, they can be planted out.

I like to keep a close eye on my plants and to select the best. To that end, large chunks of our vegetable beds are commandeered and filled with astrantias. There are other plants there too, revelling in the rich soil until they have reached sufficient bulk to be divided and planted out into the garden. The only way to get to know a plant really well is through growing it.

Occasionally we sow seed from named *Achillea millefolium* hybrids in the hope of something special turning up. These highly coloured hybrids between the common yarrow and *A. taygetea* are popular for use in prairie or natural plantings to which they lend themselves perfectly. Most qualify as bread-and-butter plants *par excellence*. They increase well on thin, poor, dry soils. Given lush growing conditions, they burgeon, making large, flat heads on strong stems, but their very vigour can cause their downfall. If a summer of over-exuberant growth is followed by a wet, cold winter, they may succumb. Best to treat them badly, or at least ignore them.

With full sun and excellent drainage, *Achillea* will go on happily for years. If clumps become congested, they can easily be pulled apart (spring is best), their old woody centres discarded and the new pieces planted in ordinary garden soil – without fuss and definitely without rich food! When replanting, use them generously and plant in swathes. One at a time or in neat groups of three, they look uncomfortable and inhibited. They should always be given the opportunity to exhibit their easy-going nature and their true personality – the *joie de vivre* that makes the bread-and-butter plants essential ingredients throughout the growing season.

3.

Shooting stars

Left

*The chalices of
Colchicum speciosum
bob up among ferns and
geraniums in the autumn
garden at Great Dixter in
East Sussex. Colchicums
are best set amongst
ground-covering plants
which will hide their nude
stems and support their
large goblets.*

Plants that contribute a fleeting sparkle to reliable beds
and borders lift the spirits and lighten the heart. They may
be here today and gone tomorrow, but however short-lived
their show they make their presence felt. Shooting stars are
the plants that cause you to catch your breath when you come
across them suddenly, or to stamp your foot when you realize
you have missed their oh-so-brief performance. So why
bother growing them at all? A garden without them is a more
predictable place – and a much duller one. They add flashes
of excitement, moments of ecstasy. Some are exquisite, some
are gorgeous and a few are downright shocking. However
short their stay, their impact is unforgettable.

MANY PERENNIALS HAVE SMALL FLOWERS clustered together in umbels or along stems, creating colourful conglomerations. Sometimes big, ostentatious flowers are a welcome change. The flamboyant blooms of oriental poppies turn heads and grab the attention of all who see them, however fleeting their show. They are archetypal shooting stars, bringing excitement to its zenith for a short time, only to disappear at a moment's notice.

The biggest and surely one of the best is the blood-red *Papaver orientale* 'Beauty of Livermere', or *P. orientale* Goliath Group as it must now be called. Doesn't have quite the same ring to it, does it? This plant is, or these plants are, very similar to the wild *P. bracteatum*, now called *P. orientale* var. *bracteatum*, a plant of sun-baked Turkish slopes. Basal foliage shows up early in the year. At this stage it makes neat rosettes. It is overtaken by the earliest performers – tulips or camassia, sweet rocket or anchusa. Without warning the poppy rapidly thrusts up its fat buds wreathed in hairy cases until, one morning, the first case splits and the red, crumpled, papery petals tumble out, unwilling to wait a moment longer, insistent that their time has come. Within hours the bud cases have been abandoned, thrown to the ground or occasionally still hanging on to one petal before it, too, swells to take its place, its puckered surface extending almost visibly, pulled to a smooth, satiny shine. The flower stems are strong and tall, up to 1.2m/4ft, and each supports a single magnificent bloom, blood red and boldly imprinted at the base of each petal with a jet black splodge. The stamens, arranged in a broad circle around the dark, central knob, are topped with an abundance of dark anthers quivering with purple pollen. As fast as the flowers come, they disappear. Each lasts a few days at the most and, although one established clump may produce scores of flowers, each individual makes its own statement. There may be a climax with ten or twenty open at one time. If these are seen against a green background, the effect is retina-searing. Once finished, they are a mess and their untidy departure is often cause for complaint. I don't know what all the fuss is about. Shearing the whole clump back to ground level will rejuvenate it. Once again there will be neat rosettes and, with a bit of luck, more flowers in late summer.

Gardening writers from Miss Jekyll onwards have exercised their minds on the subject of what should fill the holes left by the poppies. Self-supporting *Aster divaricatus* is an ideal candidate as it never lies all over the poppies but is poised just above their basal leaves. Sometimes distraction is a satisfactory option. A large clay pot, or several if there is room, can be placed close to the butchered poppies without actually being on top of them. These pots might be full of summer-flowering bulbs – lilies, *Gladiolus callianthus* or their ilk – or something with crisp, new foliage, such as a hosta or a bold grass. *Arundo donax* var. *versicolor* is ideal to distract attention and change the emphasis of the planting. *Geranium* x *oxonianum* varieties, which can be thuggish in the open border, behave impeccably confined to a pot. They have such

Right
Papaver orientale *'Derwisch': the abrasive bud cases of oriental poppies contrast with the tissue-paper petals they encase. When the moment arrives, they burst asunder and fall to the ground.*

Left

The flowers of Papaver
orientale *'Patty's Plum'
embody passion and
intrigue, adding drama
and a sense of brooding
excitement, if only for a
few days.*

a long flowering period as to go on making themselves useful for months. If you want extra foliage interest too, then *G.* x *oxonianum* 'Walter's Gift' has the added bonus of chocolate-splodged leaves in delightful contrast to its heavily veined, pale pink flowers.

At Glebe Cottage Plants, we have had to grow perennials in pots for years. Each time we exhibit at the Chelsea Flower Show or any other major show, we transport our 'garden' in pots. We use loam-based compost and plastic pots, which are ugly but retain moisture while providing good drainage. Regular watering and feeding are essential for pot-grown plants and providing them is a very enjoyable way of keeping in touch. The ones with fibrous roots thrive best confined in containers. They can reach their full potential in a pot, the fine roots exploring every corner and gathering nutrients. We use especially deep pots for perennials with tap roots, such as *Anchusa azurea* 'Loddon Royalist'. This lovely perennial borage gets frustrated and becomes stunted if its roots are unable to delve deeply into the soil. How could anyone not ensure that this plant has whatever it needs to produce its big heads of royal blue – the ultimate ultramarine?

There are so many exciting oriental poppies which bloom in early summer but none is more glamorous and showy than *Papaver orientale* 'Patty's Plum'. She has to be the true *femme fatale* of the group. Her darkness and mystery are further dramatized when surrounded by the jagged icy foliage of artichokes or cardoons or the silver lace of artemisias. Some complain about the way in which the colour fades from her deliciously damsony petals and becomes tinged with brown, just before they fall. Who cares how disgracefully she dies when she lives so exuberantly?

There are poppies for every taste. No one had better taste than the artist–gardener who gave his name to *Papaver orientale* 'Cedric Morris'. Its opulent, dusty-pink flowers with slightly ruffled petals, each with a huge bluish-black splodge at its base, are worth camping out to see in their first emerging glory. Plant breeders are busy creating varieties with stronger stems, unusual petal shapes and distinctive colours. Each year there are new ones for us to inspect or try. 'John III' is a good example with upright flowers of a clear translucent red held erect on 60cm/2ft stems. 'Aglaja', despite its commendable habit – only 60cm/2ft tall and strong-stemmed – is completely over the top with large, luscious, wavy-edged flowers in soft coral pink. The artist, the pope and the belly dancer have all won the RHS Award of Garden Merit.

You can make more of your oriental poppies by taking root cuttings. This method of propagation exploits the plants' own propensity to form new plants from every scrap of root broken off or left behind when plants are moved. Once most tap-rooted plants are established it is impossible to eliminate them. Take 2.5cm/1in sections of thick tap root (you need not lift the plant; simply remove the soil alongside it and cut off one or two likely-looking roots). Push the sections, topside up, around the edge of a pot filled with gritty compost. Water and wait. When new shoots have emerged, wait

Right
*Iris 'Harmony' is a
bulbous Reticulata iris
that brings a splash of
unexpected blue in
midwinter. Its jewel-like
colour looks even more
intense when the flowers
appear through snow.*

a little longer (new roots are made just after new shoots), pot individually
and plant out when they have formed a good root system.

Irises, too, burst upon the garden scene, only to vanish in a flash. This is
a huge group of plants, with species for every kind of situation in colours
which cover the spectrum. Their graceful flowers, many intricately marked
and ornately patterned, are fascinating but fleeting, never lasting more than
a day or two. To forgo them because of the brevity of their flowering would
be as unthinkable as banning butterflies from the garden.

Life would be poorer without the velvety darkness of black *Iris
chrysographes* or the brilliant bi-colours of *Iris* 'Rajah'. These are the plants
which make the difference between the mediocre and the unforgettable.
Iris chrysographes is a slender, elegant Asiatic iris whose flower colour varies
through red, crimson and maroon to almost black. It is the black form that
holds the greatest magnetism for most gardeners – and what a strong pull
it is too. Both standards and falls are rich deep purple, but they are so dark
that their true colour can be detected only with the strong backlighting of
dawn or dusk shining through the velvety petals.

Very dark flowers are always difficult to see and, without careful
consideration of their placing and their partners, they can become so many
shadows. A pale background formed by a froth of *Crambe cordifolia* or
Gypsophila throws the black iris flowers into sharp relief, but because both
have a multitude of tiny flowers whose white is mixed with plenty of green
from stems and leaves such a combination would never be too stark. Other
associations are even more subtle – surrounded by the sienna fuzz of
emerging bronze fennel, the vivid green verticals of stem, leaf and bud
contrast with its colour, while the flower shape is distinct against the froth
of the fennel.

The bright green, pointed buds of *Iris chrysographes* contrast perfectly
with the arching falls of the open flowers which hang down languorously,
oblivious of the 'oohs' and 'ahs' of spectators. Its fleeting display is soon over
and its linear leaves and swelling seed pods are quickly lost in the encroaching
aniseed clouds. This is a fibrous-rooted iris, easy to grow in any reasonable
soil and tolerating wet conditions well.

Germanic or bearded irises prefer a drier, open aspect where their tubers
can bask in the sun. There are thousands of named varieties, divided into three
classes: dwarf, intermediate and tall. But short or tall, flounced or plain, they
all share one characteristic – a brief but glorious flowering. Some gardeners
see the solution to the ephemerality of their display in lumping them together
in an iris garden or a special bed, as E. A. Bowles did at Myddleton House in
Enfield, where their glory is concentrated and can be enjoyed undiluted by
other plants. It is certainly easier to cultivate them in this way. A strict regime
of weeding between the plants, ensuring that their fat tubers absorb the
maximum sunshine and enabling easy excavation when the time comes
to divide and replant, is more easily followed when the plants are together.

Which iris to choose from the hundreds on offer? Whatever will give
maximum sparkle during its brief performance. There is *Iris* 'Rajah', with
yellow standards and maroon falls, or if you want something more subtle *Iris*
'Kent Pride' is beautifully marked in shades of brown. This is the sort of
exquisite flower you could contemplate for a whole day. But not longer. Each
is at its peak for such a short time. One of the most difficult exhibits to mount
at a flower show must be those of bearded irises. To watch the girls and boys
from Kelways nursery in Somerset as they painstakingly prepare their exhibit
with each bloom carefully wrapped in cotton wool is to witness true devotion.
If the weather is too warm, the flowers try to break free of their soft overcoats.
If it is too cold, out come the hairdryers to coax each fat bud into flowering
perfection to coincide with the judges' visit and the royal tour. The glory is
almost as brief in a garden setting, but each stem bears one or two auxiliary
buds which will provide a few secondary flowers. As with all shooting stars,
the point is to make the most of them while they are there.

The same goes for all other irises. In the darkest days of midwinter the first
flowers of the Algerian iris, *I. unguicularis*, can make all the difference to the
gardening psyche at its lowest ebb. Varieties of *I. reticulata* and *I. histrioides*,
from similarly sun-baked sites, have vivid, jewel-like flowers. Of all the
charming, little irises, one of them stands out for me. *Iris* 'Katharine Hodgkin'
(Reticulata) is ice blue with both standards and falls decorated with darker
blue lines in abstract patterns and the falls liberally splashed with chrome
yellow and deep blue at their centres. Her stems are very short, just long
enough to lift the big flowers above the ground or push them through the
snow. Again she prefers a poor, well-drained site.

There are other plants whose fleeting flowers are accompanied by
outstanding foliage which goes on giving its all long after petals fade and fall.
Peonies are a perfect example. The tree-and-shrub brigade can be very
unkind about peonies, deriding the brevity of their flowering and dismissing
them as barely worth growing because of it. How can they bear to turn their
backs on these most exquisite flowers? Fat, round buds, fastidiously wrapped
like some extra-special present which must be kept tightly sealed until the
specified date, soar on their stout stems, yielding their contents only at the
allotted moment. At first they look as though they will never open, as though
each one has been encased in resin or wax, but when the time comes it takes
no more than a few days for the buds to transform themselves into huge,
voluptuous globes. To begin with there is nothing to see but the vestige
of a frill, peeping out from its polished case. Within hours the whole negligée
is on display in all its gorgeousness. Take it while it is on offer, drink it in and
worship it. Too soon the flowers will overblow and disintegrate, their petals
falling to the ground.

There are peonies and there are peonies. The new growth of *Paeonia
mlokosewitschii* and the buds which rapidly appear in its midst are not shiny
at all, but tender, soft and blushing. They are shockingly new and flesh pink,

Right

*All peonies are ephemeral
and the brevity of the
performance heightens
appreciation. In* Paeonia
mlokosewitschii *the
exquisitely curved petals
encase their golden
treasure – a mass of
closely packed stamens.*

and look so vulnerable and innocent that you want to wrap them up and protect them from harm. But their appearance belies their toughness. This is a plant from the Caucasus where it lives high up in sunny forest clearings. Emulating these conditions, planting in pockets of rich soil and giving it a well-drained position in sun or dappled shade, will, in time, be repaid with generous dividends of unimpeachable foliage and a wealth of pale, perfect flowers. The lemon petals form upward-facing globes cradling a mass of quivering anthers encrusted with deeper yellow pollen.

All single peonies share this abundance of stamens and it is a characteristic too of other members of Ranunculaceae – hellebores and trollius are two familiar examples. Pollination of some species peonies results in the formation of exciting fat seed pods which burst asunder to reveal, in the case of *Paeonia mlokosewitschii*, plump, orange seeds lying in canoes lined with red velvet. Many of the species from Europe, Asia and North America also have glorious foliage. Often glaucous and velvety on emerging, later in the season it turns to red and crimson, adding a glamorous and unexpected touch.

Romneya coulteri also has a boss of golden stamens. Its white, crumpled petals burst forward from bristly buds, expanding in the sunshine until they reach saucer size. The texture is silky and the scent delicious. Despite their volume, the flowers have an airiness and lightness which makes each one precious, miraculous. Each lasts one or two days, but on a well-established plant, growing happily, hundreds may be produced. The effect is mesmerizing.

Many gardeners, me included, have trouble in getting *Romneya coulteri* established. Once it has taken hold there is no stopping it. Its roots travel underground and new shoots may appear feet away from the original plant. There seems to be a gardening law which dictates that the harder a plant is to get going, the more difficult it will be to eradicate later. Acanthus and lily of the valley are two familiar examples. *Romneya coulteri* is light and airy and innocent. There are other ephemerals which are not! *Dracunculus vulgaris*, the dragon arum, is just about as opposite as it could be, dark and menacing, the vampire to the romneya's pure maiden. The only characteristic they share is the fleeting nature of their display. *Dracunculus vulgaris* is an aroid and, in common with the rest of its family, is pollinated by flies. To attract them it emits a foul smell akin to that of rotting meat. Who said everything in the garden was lovely?

Why grow dracunculus? Despite the smell, it has its own sinister attraction. The first sign of the plant is a series of sharply pointed buds piercing the ground in a disquieting sort of a way. They are darkly mottled and reptilian and rapidly shoot up to form tall stems which support arcs of glossy, dark green leaves. From the centre of the clump of leaves rises the flower, tall, tightly wrapped and tapered. This bud may sit around for days or even weeks, pointing at the sky, swelling imperceptibly. Its unfurling is always unexpected but easily detected by the smell. The big, velvety spathe unrolls to expose the vertical spadix. Both spadix and spathe are a dark, rich crimson, the spadix

Left
The elongated urns of Arisaema consanguineum *are carefully designed to lure and capture pollinating insects. Despite their sombre colouring, they attract most gardeners too.*

Above right
Every aspect of Dracunculus vulgaris *is dangerous and otherworldly and even the stems have reptilian markings. No wonder its alias is dragon arum.*

so dark that sometimes it is almost black. Within days both smell and flower have disappeared, which is a relief and a disappointment. Graham Stuart Thomas says that 'heads of scarlet berries usually mature'. My plants have never set fruit but it must be an added excitement when it happens. Perhaps mine are in too much shade; the dragon arum is a Mediterranean plant and likes a well-drained, sunny position.

Another aroid, *Arisaema consanguineum*, grows in its native China in a wide variety of situations. Sometimes it thrusts through parched ground on sun-soaked slopes; sometimes its strange spears push through leaf mould in dark, out-of-the-way corners. Wherever it emerges it does so rapidly, opening out its whorl of leaves only when it reaches its ultimate 1.2m/4ft. Once it has attained full height, it looks so statuesque it seems permanent. The leaves form a plateau at the top of the stem. According to Dan Hinkley, who has met the plant frequently in the wild, there may be as few as seven or as many as twenty leaflets forming this parasol. Each has a long, fine tip and the spathe makes a hood which is drawn out into an even longer, attenuated tail, like a stroke from a calligrapher's brush. The spathe varies in colour from green to maroon, with narrow and paler stripes that enhance its slender urn shape. The glory of leaves and flower is fleeting. Both shrivel and even the supporting stem lasts only long enough to carry the fruits until they begin to ripen, orange and red, gradually leaning over and collapsing to bring its harvest to ground level.

Like many shooting stars, *Arisaema consanguineum* and *Dracunculus* flower in the summer. *Colchicum*, however, take the garden by storm for a few days in the autumn. Whereas *Dracunculus* announces its dangerous nature, the soft, rounded chalices of *Colchicum* belie the fact that it is an extremely poisonous plant.

Right
Colchicum speciosum
*'Album': the perfection of
its pure white chalices is
without rival. E. A.
Bowles reports seeing it in
the Backhouse Nursery in
York when there were only
three bulbs in existence
and, he says, 'They were
worth their weight in
banknotes'. Nowadays we
can all afford a few bulbs
and, since this colchicum
increases well, they are a
good investment.*

The many vernacular names for *Colchicum autumnale* – naked ladies among them – suggest that the meadow saffron was common at one time. No longer. Its former homes have been laid waste and, as with so many other disappearing plants, it is best represented in our gardens. In fact, *Colchicum* are easy enough to cultivate. They thrive in deep loam, but any sunny spot with a decent depth of soil is suitable. Whether you buy them in growth or as dry bulbs, they should be planted deeply, with at least 7–10cm/3–4in of soil above the top of the bulb. The copious summer foliage must never be trimmed off: the bulbs need all that goodness to be returned for their next performance. Lank leaves can easily be tucked away.

Most of the showy *Colchicum* that grace our autumn gardens are hybrids of *C. speciosum*. There are several good named varieties. Only a few nurseries offer them for sale in pots, but wherever possible it is best to select your plants in flower. *Colchicum* 'Rosy Dawn' is recommended for beginners, since it bulks up well in the garden. Its flowers are lilac pink with a white throat and gently tessellated. Most gardeners are turned on by the strikingly pure form of single varieties such as *C.* 'Violet Queen' and *C.* 'William Dykes'. Others prefer the double-flowered varieties. *Colchicum* 'Waterlily', a starburst of clear lilac, slender petals, is too fussy for me. Give me *C. s.* 'Atrorubens' which has especially deep crimson purple flowers. It is reasonably easy, although slow to increase.

One of the most pondered puzzles in gardening is what to grow with *Colchicum* to hide the shocking nudity of their stems and to offer support for their somewhat wobbly legs. They need to be able to push through the supporting cast, but in its turn the ground cover must be able to breathe when the substantial leaves of its basement-dwelling neighbours shoot through in spring and die gracelessly in summer. Short cranesbills, such as forms of *Geranium sanguineum*, are ideal, 'Album' being the best because its stems are more wiry than the others and offer better scaffolding. The foliage of evergreen *Epimedium* x *versicolor* or its lovely twin cultivars, 'Sulphureum' and 'Neosulphureum', provides a vivid green backdrop to the flowers of any of the stronger *Colchicum speciosum* forms. The large, silver, furry lambs' lugs of *Stachys byzantina* make a perfect foil both in texture and colour to the raging puce of some *Colchicum*. Reginald Farrer describes *Colchicum* as having 'an evil colour'. Silvery foliage always helps neutralize painful colours. Even if the *Stachys* is temporarily overcome by the *Colchicum*'s palm-like leaves, it is too tough a plant to suffer anything more than a temporary setback.

Whether *Colchicum* or poppies, irises or dragon arums, shooting stars contribute flashes of brilliance whose very transience quickens the garden's pulse and elevates prose to poetry.

4.

Will-o'-the-wisps & wafty whisperers

Left
Backlit by evening sun, the dancing heads of Spanish oats, Stipa gigantea, *bring levity and movement to this late-summer scene.*

One of the reasons we love plants so much is that they are alive, growing and changing constantly. None more so than will-o'-the-wisps and wafty whisperers, the plants that bring rustling rhythms and sparkling lights. They add the touch of frivolity needed in beds and borders where, despite careful planning, wise plant choice and the creation of cultivational nirvana, there is still something lacking. Clumps of stalwart plants may be complementing each other beautifully, enriched by fleeting visits from shooting stars, but the borders seem too static, too staid. There may be exciting combinations of colour and form, drama queens may sit around demanding to be admired, but despite their insistence that we need look no further an extra dimension is needed. Here are plants that add sound, light and movement when things have become too serious.

75

THE REASSURANCE OF A STATIC GARDEN where everything is clipped and controlled and clumpy can never compare to the thrill of a place which includes plants that, energized by the elements, scintillate and shimmer. The more restricted the space, the more imperative it is to liven it up. Tall grasses are some of the most animated of plants. Of these, varieties of the blue moor grass, *Molinia caerulea*, offer a comprehensive range. Each has its own personality and best uses. Small gardens could not accommodate some of the more voluminous cultivars, but *M. caerulea* subsp. *caerulea* 'Edith Dudszus' has vertical, needle-like foliage and refined, upright flower stems, making her just the right candidate for a tight spot. Several plants could be used about 60cm/2ft apart, close to the convergence of two paths where height is needed but overhanging growth would be impractical. Despite the sentinel effect, you can see through 'Edith Dudszus', glimpsing treats in store as you walk along the path.

Such grasses give versatility to small spaces. If they have more than one guise, their metamorphosis changes the picture again. All *Molinia* start blue, purple and green but change to gold in the autumn. This late transformation is especially effective when backlit at dawn or dusk. Stems and seed heads glow as though imbued with some internal light. *Molinia caerulea* subsp. *arundinacea* 'Windspiel' (Wind Games) does just what its name denotes, moving playfully this way and that with every breeze. It is too expansive for small gardens, but given its head in a broad border it animates the scene. The aptly named 'Transparent' is just as big, but it has such a dainty demeanour that it would not be out of place in a small space. As the name suggests it is see-through and a host of other plants may be accommodated around its skirts. Its elegant, arching stems twinkle with thousands of tiny flowers and, as they turn to seed, the tips of the stems bend even closer towards the ground.

Molinia caerulea is happiest out in the open. For a light touch in a shady place, there is the wood mellick, *Melica unifora, w*ith dainty inflorescences composed of small individual flowers.

Deschampsia flexuosa, the wavy hair grass, makes vivid acid green fountains in the spring and combines beautifully with the lemon buttercup, *Ranunculus acris* 'Citrinus', and the stiff, near-turquoise spikes of *Veronica gentianoides*. Its dainty, pink-tinged flowers are lustrous, gathering light from all around and providing at the height of their charming performance a counterpoint to the voluptuous flowers of oriental poppies. The very best combination is with the dirty crimson, rippled heads of *Papaver orientale* 'Patty's Plum' floating above dense clouds of the fairy grass.

Many grasses have a dreamy insubstantiality which defies definition. A meadow in full flight is a sea of lilting movement, without focal points. In a garden this effect can be harnessed in smaller areas with a limited palette of plants. If you were keen to ring the changes and prefer to use annuals and tender plants, small dahlias could mix with *Hordeum jubatum* sown direct

Right
On tall stems the tiny individual flowers of blue moor grass, Molinia caerulea *subsp.* arundinacea *'Transparent', catch the light like drops of dew. When flowers turn to seed, the effect persists, although the wiry, pliant stems bow over with the increased weight.*

Left

At close quarters the awns of Hordeum jubatum *are seen to be closely packed and parallel like a formal hair-do depicted on the walls of an Egyptian tomb. En masse the effect of foxtail barley is light and lilting, pitched this way and that in constant motion.*

after the dahlia tubers have been planted. The two will intermingle happily, the foxtail barley moving gently, now exposing the flowers, now obscuring them with an almost filmic quality.

Stipa calamagrostis is one of the waftiest of grasses. Both its silky inflorescence and its fluffy seed heads provide a lightness of touch which can lift even a stodgy planting to a happier level. Some of the smaller varieties of *Stipa* have soft flowers and seed heads too. One vernacular name for *S. arundinacea* is tress grass because of its long, soft inflorescence. Planted on top of a wall or in a tall pot, the grass can demonstrate this characteristic most effectively, its long, soft flowers floating down to ground level like Rapunzel's locks. Another name for this plant is pheasant grass. Its blades, like the bird's plumage, are a lustrous mixture of olive green, henna red and bronze. In shade its colouring is more subdued, though still rich. In full sun, given good soil, it is at its most vivid. Despite its antipodean origins, in thin, dry soils, many blades may dry out, giving its tussocks a desiccated look. In such soils incorporate plenty of humus at planting time. *Stipa arundinacea* is evergreen and as with all evergreen grasses it should never be cut back. Teasing out dead stems is the best way to deal with excessive thatch and old flowers. Even when they do not result in death, drastic haircuts will maim evergreen grasses.

Stipa gigantea sometimes loses all its basal foliage during the winter. Even when it retains a central clump of greenery, all the dross from the year's growth should be pulled away. This is a plant of sun-baked Iberian hillsides. Its common name is Spanish oats and though it will tolerate cold winter temperatures, zone 7, it will turn up its toes if expected to put up with wet feet too. Although its tall, stiff stems are magnificent at the end of the season with their branching heads transformed to gold, it has more mobility and grace earlier in the year. The first flower buds start to emerge as the weather warms up. It is at this stage you dash out to count them and anticipate the glory they will soon provide. As the stems lengthen, the tightly packed inflorescence pulls itself from the fattened flower stems like some emerging insect, lengthening and shaking itself out until the long, drooping panicles are released and shake their willowy heads freely in the soft summer air. At this time too there is a magical silvery iridescence about the flower heads, heightened by the tiny, golden pollen grains which decorate the new flowers. Wafty or what?

There are many other tall grasses which add a light touch. The pampas grasses, forms of *Cortaderia* from South America, had become a figure of fun among the gardening elite. Planted in lonely isolation as a focal point in highly manicured lawns in small suburban gardens, they became a symbol of all that was artificial and downright daft about 1950s and 60s gardens. To disenfranchize a plant and ban it because it has been abused is the worst sort of gardening bigotry. Thankfully, thinking gardeners realize how beautiful some forms of pampas can be and what their gardens might miss without them. Once again their star is in the ascendant.

Right

Cortaderia selloana
*'Rendatleri' is one of the
most elegant varieties of
pampas grass, its plumes
responding to every breath
of wind. Integrated in beds
and borders, rather than
isolated as though it had
done something wrong,
pampas grass adds a
wafty fanfare to the
autumn garden.*

Cortaderia selloana 'Pumila' is a compact variety (still tall at 1.8m/6ft) with closely packed, creamy plumes. *Cortaderia selloana* 'Monstrosa', at the other end of the scale, can reach 3m/10ft. Its plumes are open, airy – and huge. The striking *C. s.* 'Rendatleri' is even more imposing and its huge plumes, borne on one side of the 3m/10ft stems, are soft pink. All these flower late in the year and, although they can be spoilt by early gales, for the most part they will reach their zenith without undue damage, their tall standards bringing a final touch of the light fantastic to the dwindling autumnal pageant.

Thalictrum delavayi is a wafty plant. It forms a basal clump of fine 'maidenhair' foliage from which the flower stalks almost magically emerge, shooting up and branching as they go, flinging out caulescent leaves at every change of direction. Eventually, after it has formed a graceful framework, the buds emerge at the tips of each stem. At first green and clustered, they separate, each with its own slender, wiry stem, and change to lilac. The buds are slender, too, and reminiscent of clematis on a tiny scale. Each one unfolds into a perfect parasol and the creamy-white anthers which dangle from the pendulous stamens complete the quivering charm. The foliage and stems start green but soon assume purple tinges. The best foliage and stem colour often results from stress and pot-grown plants in full sun are sometimes completely purple, leaves and all.

A mature, well-grown *Thalictrum delavayi* will flower for several weeks, the apical buds opening first, followed by the supporting cast on the subsidiary stems. If the weather is cool, the display can last much longer. Almost imperceptibly the petals fall, giving way to clusters of deep purple seed pods which bring a different, more subtle decorative quality to the plant. The seed-laden stems are particularly effective in silhouette, although the flowers are best seen against a dark background. This presents a bit of a 'where to plant?' conundrum. There are plenty of solutions, though. An east–west bed with a hedge or fence to the north or south would allow appreciation of both flowers and fruit. Later still the foliage changes to amber yellow, an exciting contrast against the dark stalks. In its native habitat the plant's height is between 60cm/2ft and 1.8m/6ft. In gardens, too, its stature is affected by the cultural conditions, soil, moisture and available light. My first meeting with it was in late summer at Marwood Hill, Devon, where it was planted close to a wall at the back of a dense, mixed border. It was 2.4m/8ft high, politely waving its diaphanous, flower-studded stems as if anxious not to be overlooked: unmissable despite the competition.

A hum of excitement rippled through the plant world when Bledwyn Wynn-Jones from Crûg Farm Plants in Wales introduced a new form of *Thalictrum delavayi*. In a consignment of plants from China were a few plants labelled 'Thalictrum decorum'. Bledwyn grew these on and was delighted. From such a discriminating nurseryman with a treasure trove of fine plants, this is high praise. The plant is now recognized as a variety of *T. delavayi* and called *T. delavayi* var. *decorum*. What's the difference? It is smaller in all its parts than

the type. Both flowers and foliage are finer and the fuzzy, ephemeral effect is even more distinctive. Its buds are slightly longer and the 'pixie hat' similarity as the flowers open is even more marked. It also seems to flower later – in our garden it creates a purple haze from July till late September.

The shape of diaphanous thalictrums is spoiled by heavy-handed staking. It is important to allow such plants to be themselves. Give it the protection of a more substantial neighbour on its windward side and plant it among herbaceous plants that can lend it a shoulder to lean on. The whole idea is that it should mingle and spread its happy, carefree quality into the most sombre corners. A member of the buttercup family, Ranunculaceae, it grows high up on open hillsides in scrub and at the edge of woods in northwest Yunnan. The ground is often steep, stony and acid. You would expect a buttercup to need more moisture, but this is provided in its west China home by cloud cover and high humidity. It is impossible to replicate these conditions exactly, but the plant seems to succeed in a broad range of situations. Any reasonable soil will do in a sunny position or in dappled shade. Adequate drainage is essential.

Gaura lindheimeri, a member of Onagraceae, the willow-herb family, is another representative of the diaphanous detachment. It is a charming, wistful plant which flowers indefatigably throughout the summer, producing literally hundreds of its pretty, white flowers along tall, willowy stems. The individual flowers are small with bigger petals at the top which make it look as though the whole plant had been settled by flocks of butterflies. When the breeze blows the slender stems back and forth, it is easy to imagine the whole lot fluttering upwards in a cloud only to settle again a moment later.

Right

*The strong, wiry stems
of* Gillenia trifoliata *are
bedecked with starry,
white flowers, creating
a nebulous effect.*

Hailing from the western United States of America, *Gaura* is reasonably hardy but has a reputation for being short-lived. It hates winter wet, but is also devastated by droughty conditions in the summer. There is a deep-pink-flowered variety called *G. lindheimeri* 'Siskiyou Pink' which is not such a lovely mover, being much shorter than the species.

Another North American plant superficially similar to *Gaura* is *Gillenia trifoliata*. It is one of the most delightful plants in the garden and always initiates a smile, even from the grumpiest person in their gloomiest mood. Its wiry, reddish stems branch this way and that, giving it a shrubby appearance. During late summer these are scattered with dainty, white stars. *Gillenia* belongs to the rose family and its petals fall just as quickly as those of a single rose. Luckily there is a succession of flowers over a few weeks, although I would still worship it if its flowering lasted only a day. Despite being a woodlander, it will grow happily in an open border alongside clumps of larger, heavier plants whose weight is lifted by its light, airy presence. In autumn the whole bush turns to glowing reds and oranges.

On a much grander scale, *Crambe cordifolia* provides a similarly elegant effect. Its big cabbage leaves of dark green are unprepossessing and take up too much space but are completely forgotten when the huge, branching flower stems launch themselves upwards in early summer. The tiny, white flowers scattered through them create a 'Milky Way' impression. These great, nebulous clouds emit the sweetest scent. The flowers of most crucifers have beautiful perfume – and almost all their leaves have the opposite! Brassicas like lime, but *C. cordifolia* will thrive on any fertile soil. It is worth working in a dressing of lime or calcified seaweed to heavy, acid clay soil before planting.

Gypsophila is often called the 'chalk plant' and is quite literally in its element when growing on chalk or any other light alkaline soil. Although we have grown it on neutral to acid clay, it has never lasted for more than a season. When happy it creates billowing, misty clouds of white and pink. Let them roll in to cover the demise of early poppies and the corpses of spring bulbs. The framework that remains after the flowers have faded can be used as scaffolding for clambering annuals, such as ipomoea or nasturtiums.

The structure of *Gypsophila* and *Crambe* is complex but open. There are other plants which create a nebulous effect in a different way. *Sedum* are succulent and solid, yet the substantial flower heads of some varieties, and the manner in which the individual flowers open, create depth and volume that can produce a 'cloudy' effect, especially when seen from a distance. A bank of *Sedum* 'Strawberries and Cream' overlooked by fluffy seed heads of *Stipa calamagrostis* conjures up a late-afternoon sky with dark cumulus on the horizon and above them mares' tails, moving and changing in the upper atmosphere.

Not everything wafty is voluminous. Indispensable light touches are made by smaller plants closer to ground level which lift low plantings and create a spumy effect along the edges of flowerbeds. Some are annuals or biennials.

Left
Omphalodes cappadocica
*'Starry Eyes' softens edges
in a shady situation.*
Right
*The ornate flowers of love-
in-a-mist,* Nigella
damascena, *are soft blue
touched with green,
floating above
diaphanous green ruffs.*

Love-in-a-mist, *Nigella damascena*, is one of the frothiest of plants. Mingling into surrounding greenery, it makes the planting float. Its relatively large flowers add to the impression as they hover above the fuzzy leaves. With forget-me-nots, it is the flowers that provide the froth. Would tulips look so substantial without the low-lying mist of *Myosotis* swirling around them?

Omphalodes linifolia is another borage relative which produces the froth effect. It loves sunshine and relishes heat. Its narrow, rounded, glaucous leaves make springy cushions for thousands of dimpled, white flowers. The seed too is dimpled (*Omphalodes* comes from the Greek for navel), and it is easy to raise plants from seed sown early in the year. The seed is big, so can be station sown, one or two seeds to each compartment in a module tray. Plants can be potted on individually until frost is past or in mild areas they can be planted directly into the soil. For a hot, dry garden this has to be one of the best plants for softening edges, growing alongside dianthus and with the glaucous, wavy leaves of *Crambe maritima* in the background. The sea-kale has alyssum-like, sweetly scented flowers clustered more densely along stout, branching stems. *Omphalodes cappadocica* is a perennial and brings the same sort of effect as its sun-loving cousin to the shady side of the garden, especially in the variety 'Starry Eyes' where the blue flowers are margined with pale lavender.

Whether it is groups of grasses deliberately designed to introduce lilting rhythms or the self-sown fuzz of fennel or nigella, levity, movement and music can help prevent any garden taking itself too seriously. Wafty plants may strike up secondary melodies or constitute a major theme in the symphony, changing the pace of the planting, and bringing it to life.

5.

Prickly customers & soft touches

The touchy-feely aspect of plants is often underused, even ignored in favour of more obvious qualities – structure and form and, of course, colour. While colour may evoke emotion, it is remote, whereas texture is immediate, intimate, implying physical contact between the gardener and the plant. The way something feels, or looks as though it feels, draws us close enough to touch or to examine. At summer flower shows we always put a row of *Stipa tenuissima* on the end of our sales table. As the waftiest of wafty plants, it belongs in Chapter 4, but that impression is created not only by the way it looks, but also by the way it feels, and feelings belong here. Both the people selling behind the table and those buying in front of it instinctively fondle the soft fronds. Visually and in a tactile way they engender relaxation and calm.

TEXTURE BRINGS AN EXTRA DIMENSION to our experience of gardens. Even when a plant is fiercely armed with thorns or spikes, it is the way we imagine it would feel which brings us close to it. Not too close in some cases! Plants don't come much more spiky than *Onopordon acanthium*, the Scotch thistle. It is not easy to overlook the giant rosettes which it makes in its first year, but the staggering he-man stems which rise up from its giant basal rosettes in the following year are impossible to ignore.

Onopordon acanthium cannot make up its mind where its loyalties lie. Not only are its softly fluffy leaves armed at their extremities with fierce barbs, but its spherical, cobwebby buds bristle with prickles too. In its arid home, goats do not eat it and its petals are protected from the sun. It is free to grow happily, producing flowers and setting seed, which is vitally important since it is a biennial.

Every kind of characteristic a plant possesses has evolved to deal with the specific conditions it encounters. The methods they adopt influence the shape, size and the texture of their leaves often with effects which we gardeners can exploit in the ornament of our gardens. Some of the most endearing are plants with soft, furry leaves.

Stachys byzantina, the ubiquitous lambs' lugs, is surely the most furry of plants. In our house it is known as the 'ticky plant'. Both daughters used it as a comforter when they were very young, detaching a leaf and tickling their noses with it in a state of pure ecstasy. The woolliness of the whole plant is created by thousands of tiny hairs, developed to protect the leaf cuticle from the searing sun of its high Middle Eastern home. In the garden its soft, dense clumps belie these tough-guy characteristics. Later the ground-hugging carpet takes backseat to a forest of 37cm/15in woolly flower spikes.

Several of these furry plants have more than one persona, which makes them doubly useful. The big, felted rosettes of *Salvia aethiopis* and its close cousin *S. argentea* throw up enormous, branching spikes smothered in white, hooded flowers. *Verbascum*, often uninvited but usually most welcome guests, put on a similar performance. Mullein leaves were once used to line children's shoes and it is difficult to keep your feet, let alone your hands, off their downy foliage. *Verbascum bombyciferum*, a European native, is as woolly as can be. Its leaves form huge rosettes. Their geometry is so perfect that, even when they have sprung up in a place allotted to some more permanent plant, it is difficult to bring yourself to hoick them out. There is majesty too about the reach-for-the-sky columns that shoot up in the second year.

Verbascum (Cotswold Group) 'Cotswold King' is one of my favourites. Misleadingly named to sound like one of the old Cotswold hybrids, it is for sure a species. Some botanists think it synonymous with *V. creticum* (from Crete), whereas others believe it to be a Turkish species. Whatever its provenance, it is well worth growing. It is not as soft and furry as some, nor as tall as many. Established plants will make 90cm/3ft. Its buds are fat and waxy and the flowers are large and very cheeky, set flat against the stem so

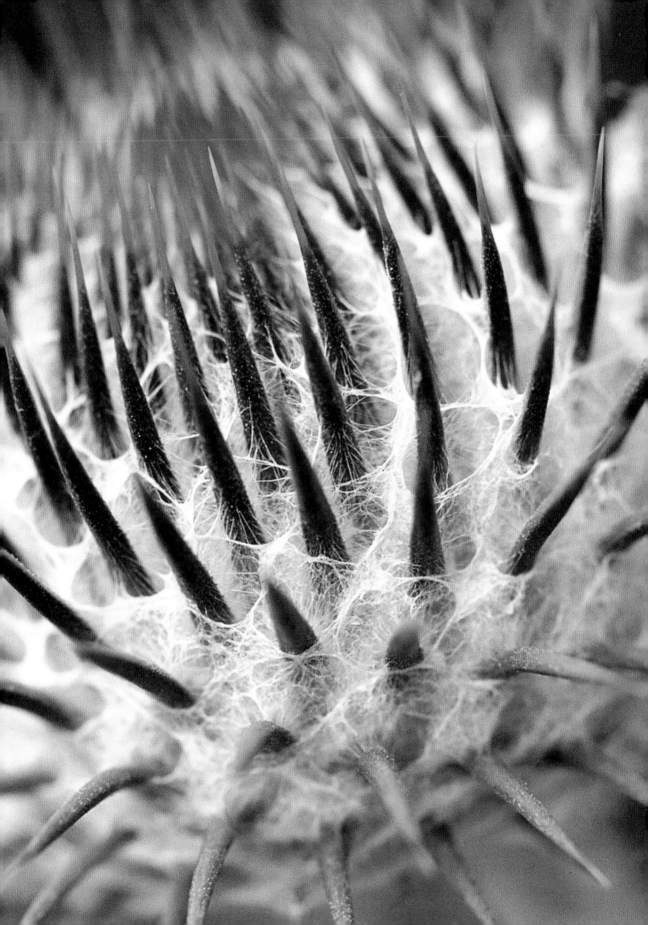

Left

The cheery yellow flowers of Verbascum *'Cotswold King' are set flat against its stems with stigma and stamens at the ready. As well as the central 'bee' there is a sharp, citric scent too. What self-respecting pollinator could resist the invitation?*

that its face looks directly at you and smiles. The colouring of the unusually large flowers is graded gently from bright chrome yellow at the top to palest lemon at the lower edge. The central 'bee', designed to attract pollinators, is insect-like, while the pistil protrudes in a long curve for all the world like a reptile's tongue. Either side of it the anthers dangle, ready to brush their pollen on any insect which has succumbed to the lure. Another ploy for successful pollination is the scent, which is outstanding, sharp and citric. It sets copious amounts of seed and like most species mulleins is a monocarpic biennial, dying after it has accomplished its purpose. In a garden setting, plants can be persuaded to last another year by cutting down the flowered stem to ground level. Growing from seed is so easy it seems a shame not to have lots of plants the next year. An early spring sowing will produce flowering plants in the same year, while plants from late sowings will flower the next. You need never be without flowering plants.

There are hundreds of *Verbascum* species from Turkey, the Middle East and the Mediterranean and many grow well in more northern latitudes provided they have poor, preferably alkaline soil and a sunny site. Most are tall and erect with the flower spike, which may branch like a huge candelabrum, rising from the centre of a large rosette of felted leaves. *Verbascum olympicum* is just as it sounds – a giant, sometimes reaching 2.4m/8ft. It would make an interesting class at the local flower show and a pleasant change from giant onions and mammoth leeks. *Verbascum bombyciferum* is more manageable and its thickly felted rosettes and woolly columns make it a very desirable subject, especially for those who enjoy touchy-feely contact.

Big softies like these can be used with similar plants deliberately to create a soothing picture. Soft grasses – *Stipa, Carex* and *Calamagrostis* – add froth while sticking to the plot. If you want height without anything too statuesque, fuzzy fennel will create a haze or the tall, wafty stems of *Molinia caerulea* subsp. *arundinacea* 'Transparent' could float overhead. All thrive in well-drained, sunny conditions.

There are furry flowers too. In *Pulsatilla vulgaris* flower, stem and petals are all covered in down. Before the flowers even think of making an appearance, the finely cut leaves materialize. They are ferny and silvered at first, emerging tentatively like inquisitive sea anemones as if to feel the air. If *Pulsatilla* is grown in the poor conditions which suit it best, the silvery sheen is at its most pronounced. All these alpine anemones relish thin, alkaline soils and love an open, sunny situation. Reginald Farrer suggests that the Romans carried *P. vulgaris* to England, perhaps unknowingly, by importing seed in lime-mortar or stone, and that many of the places where it has naturalized are the sites of former Roman earthworks. Although it will survive on richer, more fertile soil, it will not be itself. Any plant grown under conditions vastly different from those it is used to in the wild is liable to go through a personality change. The charm of *Pulsatilla* is that its growth is compact and sturdy and very silvery. A regime of rich soil and over-feeding

Right

All the surfaces of the pasque flower, Pulsatilla vulgaris, *are covered in down. Both the flowers and the fluffy seed heads which succeed them glisten on a sunny day. This plant is at its most silvery when growing in poor, well-drained soil, as it does in the wild.*

will make the leaves, flowers and seed heads unnaturally tall and weak. The plant will lose its sparkle.

The flowers of *Pulsatilla vulgaris* are fleeting, quiet and hardly noticeable in dull weather, bending their heads, each tiny hair on the outside of their petals imbued with droplets of water. When the sun begins to shine, the flowers turn their faces towards it, so many stars of rich, deep purple, each lit by a boss of golden stamens with a tufted, purple stigma at its heart. The seed heads complete the furry, fluffy cycle. They are elegant in the extreme, turning from purple to white as they age, each long tendril covered in fine fluff. When the seeds are ripe each takes off on its own parachute: the breeze catches the tiny hairs and lifts the precious package, transporting it to pastures new. At their glistening best, lit by the spring sunshine, the seed heads are easily as beautiful as the flowers.

Lupinus varius subsp. *orientalis,* an annual blue lupin, is covered in fluff from top to tail. At first it is a monochromatic picture – a striking tower of close-assembled buds coated in fine, silvery fur. As the buds begin to thrust outwards and the tower heightens, creating space between them, the colour is turned on, a rich, saturated blue. Green creeps in on stalk, calyx and leaf. Throughout its life there is a soft, downy quality about this lupin which makes you want to reach out and stroke it.

Some of my favourite plants prompt the opposite reaction. I am seldom given plants – people assume I can grow them myself since I run a nursery. One year, though, I received several plant presents. Without exception, they had spikes, barbs or thorns. I was thrilled with them all, although that thing which people say about dog-owners looking like their pets did spring to mind.

One of these gifts was a particularly blue form of *Eryngium bourgatii*. This is one of the best-armed plants around, with spiny ends to its leaves and flower bracts. The basal rosette of leaves is informal since each leaf is suspended on a slender stem radiating randomly. The leaves are of glaucous grey and are given an especially sparkling quality by the white markings which delineate the midribs and every lateral vein. They look for all the world as though some mischievous pixie had poured mercury over the leaf and that it had run along every gully and crevice.

The foliage of *Eryngium bourgatii* is as striking as its flower. On mature plants numerous flower stems are produced. Each one branches to bear five or six substantial flower heads. At first these are silvery sea green, but as the stems lengthen and the bracts enlarge, a miraculous transformation takes place. One morning there is the faintest tinge of blue. Day by day the quantity of blue increases so that eventually the flowers, bracts and the stems which support them are imbued with bright blue. There is nothing more arresting in the midsummer garden than these vivid focal points of ultramarine.

Eryngium belong to the family Apiaceae, until recently Umbelliferae. At first glimpse the family resemblance is hard to see. Take a closer look and the tiny flowers which form the central cone bear a striking similarity to the

individual florets of a head of cow-parsley or pimpinella. The separate flowers of *Astrantia* that compose the pincushion centre also have the same formation. Both *Astrantia* and all the European *Eryngium* have bracts on which the arrangement of flowers sits. In the *Astrantia* they are papery, in *Eryngium* thick and succulent, protecting the flowers until such time as they can look after themselves. After pollination the seeds become increasingly spiny. By the time they are ripe they are quite brutal. We collect seed from all our *Eryngium*, severing the flower stems and cutting the entire heads from the plant when seed is ripe. Everyone is happy to do this but when it comes to separating the spiky seed and detaching it from the even spikier seed head there is always a shortage of volunteers. The best method is to cut each stem long enough to grasp it securely while keeping the bracts at bay and to use a plastic pen top to push the seeds free. If this is performed over a piece of thick paper already folded so that the loose seed can be tipped into envelopes or bags, then injuries should be kept to a minimum.

Eryngium alpinum is a different kettle of fish. This rosette-forming sea holly is another must-have plant. Its double layer of breathtakingly blue bracts is deeply divided, making them appear fluffy. Although the ends of the bracts are pointed, the whole construction is soft to the touch. Selections of *E. alpinum* are often sold as cut flowers and many gardeners are first introduced to this plant in a bunch. It has a fascinating persona and, although difficult to find commercially, once acquired and with a modicum of soil preparation, it is long-lived. I cannot imagine any plant it would not enhance. From the lemon daisies of *Anthemis tinctoria* 'Wargrave Variety' or *A. tinctoria* 'E.C. Buxton' to the rich magenta of *Geranium psilostemon* or its yellow-leaved progeny, *G.* 'Ann Folkard', it provides an ideal partner, making every association special.

Eryngium alpinum and *E. bourgatii* are the parents of *E.* x *zabelli* which in the cultivar 'Violetta' has violet blue flowers with silvery-blue bracts. Both *E. alpinum* and *E. bourgatii* are native to the Alps and high mountains of southern Europe, Turkey and north Africa where they grow on well-drained, generally alkaline soils, always in sunny positions. My garden has heavy clay but, provided I incorporate plenty of grit and if possible old lime-mortar at planting time, sea hollies thrive and increase well year on year. Their worst enemies are stagnant, peaty soils and winter wet.

There is nothing about bear's breeches, *Acanthus spinosus* Spinosissimus Group, that you would be inclined to caress. The flowers of all acanthus are prickly and so are the leaves of most varieties. (*Acanthus mollis* is an exception, *mollis* meaning soft, and certainly the leaves have no prickles although they are no less majestic for that.) This is the plant whose leaf shape and structure inspired the carved designs atop Corinthian columns. As its name suggests, *A. spinosus* Spinosissimus Group is the prickliest and as spiny as a porcupine. What a claim to fame! Its deeply cut leaves are polished, dark viridian green with sharp spines at every edge. Now considered to be just a particularly

Right
Acanthus spinosus
disarmed! Stately flower
stems make ideal
scaffolding for spiders'
webs, which leave them
thick with silver
candyfloss. With or
without woolly overcoats,
the spikes of acanthus
are outstanding.

vicious form of *A. spinosus*, it has huge spikes of sinister, hooded flowers – white with purple bracts – up to 1.5m/5ft high. An amusing unity of opposites is created when spiders wrap their webs around the acanthus stems.

Galactites tomentosa is another sharp plant that I was given. This biennial Mediterranean thistle is a delight throughout its short life – from early rosettes to spiny, branching bushes decorated with little, pink thistles which mark its crescendo. The leaves change shape as the plant grows, becoming more slender and holly-like as it expands, sub-dividing and shooting out as it goes. The more it grows, the spikier it looks. It is now a firm favourite, if not a close friend. It is probably cursed in its native haunts where it proliferates, like most thistles, by seed carried on downy parachutes. In colder climes it sets little seed, although once you have a plant in the garden there are always a few seedlings to be found. I am delighted to discover them – small, green starfish, etched with white and pinched into little, sharp spines around their edges. If they can be left where they have decided to grow, so much the better. If not, they can be successfully transported to a chosen site, but this must be done carefully and while they are still very young.

All tap-rooted annuals and biennials resent root disturbance and if I am lucky enough to find a few seeds on my *Galactites*, they are sown individually in modules so that they can be potted on into bigger pots or planted out into the ground without distressing the plant. This is the best practice with all short-lived plants, such as annual poppies and *Orlaya grandiflora*, when they are destined for a special place or planting. Although they could be sown *in situ*, there is never any certainty about where they will pop up or even whether seed will germinate at all.

Of a similar disposition although much more generous with its self-seeding is the herb *Borago officinalis*. Borage may seem a lowly plant but its intriguing blue or white flowers with their central pointel are endearing and the hairy flower stems are entrancing covered in dew and backlit by early morning sun.

Every surface of the linear leaves of *Convolvulus cneorum* is covered in fine hair, but unlike the abrasive, sticky-out hair which covers borage stems it lies completely flat, giving each convolvulus leaf a smooth, reflective sheen, which is soft to the touch. *Convolvulus cneorum* is probably the most silver of all silver-leaved plants, bringing a sense of sun and light to the garden even on a dark day. In common with almost all silver plants it thrives on poverty and relishes sun. The white trumpet flowers with yellow centres are a bonus.

There are numerous techniques adopted by sunbathers to help them survive and flourish in an inhospitable environment. Many of these silver plants conserve water by keeping their leaf surface to a minimum. Transpiration is low and the plant conserves whatever moisture is available. Sometimes, as in the case of lavender, *Santolina* and rosemary, this is achieved by reducing the leaves to needles. In other cases, such as *Artemisia*, the leaves are very finely cut. The great, billowing, silver-filigree clumps of *A. absinthium* or *A. arborescens* are indispensable. Probably the best of all

these immensely tactile plants is *A.* 'Powis Castle', raised by Jimmy Hancock who was head gardener at Powis Castle in Welshpool, Powys, and for many years thrilled and delighted visitors with superlative displays and innovative arrangements on its broad terraces.

Artemisia alba 'Canescens' is known in the vernacular as the wire-wool bush. It reminds me of the tumbleweed which rolls around the sets of ghost towns in Westerns. Its filigree, curling leaves and silvery-white colouring give it a misty appearance from a distance. Close to they make a telling contrast with large-leaved subjects. Despite its quirkiness, or perhaps because of it, this is a very beautiful plant.

The prostrate stems of *Artemisia schmidtiana* 'Nana' are immensely strokable, softly dense and silvery. The flowers are tiny and round like small, knobbly embroidery knots along the silken strands of stems and leaves, enriching the texture here and there. With the frivolously fluffy heads of *Pennisetum alopecuroides* 'Herbstzauber' (Autumn Magic) as a backdrop and a clump or two of *Origanum* 'Kent Beauty' close by, huge restraint would be needed not to indulge in an orgy of stroking.

Shiny leaves, especially those of shade lovers, are often a device to dispel water and help plants cope with tree drip. Sometimes they are smooth and polished as in the rounded, dark green foliage of *Asarum europaeum*, the hardy wild ginger. Despite the depth of colour, the handsome leaves are reflective, almost mirror-like. Other plants have slender, grass-like foliage which quickly sheds rain. When wet the foliage of *Ophiopogon japonicus* and the closely related *Liriope muscari* glistens. Even the black, linear leaves of the ubiquitous *Ophiopogon planiscapus* 'Nigrescens' reflect any available light, especially in wet weather.

In contrast the foliage of *Rodgersia podophylla* and *R. pinnata* 'Superba' has a puckered, lacquered look. Often there is a real sheen on the new leaves as they open their great hands in spring, at this stage flushed with pink. Some become brilliantly green during the summer when tall stems bear fluffy panicles of creamy-white, pink or red flowers.

Almost all rodgersias develop scintillating autumn colour – with a gloss, as though someone had rubbed long and hard to bring them to the ultimate of shininess for their final cavalcade. Many distinguished plantsmen have made selections of *R. podophylla* and new collections from the wild are occasionally introduced to add extra polish to the gardener's textural repertoire.

The devices plants use to protect their leaves, stems and flowers are legion. This wealth of texture offers endless opportunities to add an extra dimension of rich sensuality to our planting schemes.

6.

Seductive sophisticates

Left
Paris polyphylla *is a green treasure from the forests of the Orient with a flower that lasts for several months. Who could resist its exquisite colouring and symmetry?*

Just as the visitors to an art gallery cluster around the best pictures, there are plants in our gardens that attract a crowd. These charismatic characters draw our attention and hold it effortlessly. Unlike the drama queens we will meet later (they demanded to be first but I have made them wait till the grand finale), the seductive sophisticates attract attention without making a fuss. They are the *crème de la crème*. Something about the subtlety of their colour or the poise of their bearing, the perfection of their shape or their entire persona, induces us to travel far afield to find them. Whether they are plants of shady woodland or open field, from the highest mountains or the water's edge, all have the power to induce sighs and make knees go weak. Within almost every genus there are one or two plants which possess this magical capacity.

BLUE FLOWERS ARE ALWAYS A DRAW but none has such magnetism as those whose colour reminds us of the sea and the sky. The blue Himalayan poppy, *Meconopsis betonicifolia*, is an ooh-aah plant *par excellence*. Looking into an individual flower is a revelation. Each deep cerulean blue, slightly crumpled petal is elegantly poised. As the flower opens fully the petals are stretched smooth like wet silk drying on a hot day. At the centre of their shallow cups, a boss of fine stamens, their anthers dusted in gold, surround the central stigma which thrusts itself forward, intent on pollination.

The elegant foliage, the stems and the drooping, dimpled buds are all covered in a fine, bronze fuzz designed to catch every drop of dew on the high eastern slopes of its homeland. *Meconopsis* do best where the climate is closest to their natural environment, cool and moist. High humidity and rich soil are what they need. According to the famous plant hunter George Sheriff, they should be planted on top of a dead sheep. Hmmm. Their blue is a blue to sing about. There is a host of variations on the same theme, some of even more electrifying blue than straightforward *M. betonicifolia* and plant breeders make claims and counter-claims, all asserting their hybrids and selections to be the bluest yet. *Meconopsis betonicifolia* is short-lived, often monocarpic, whereas *M. grandis* is a perennial but loath to set seed.

Meconopsis punicea is the most distinguished member of this very special family. It is notoriously difficult to grow and, although it was first introduced into cultivation in the West more than a century ago, it has been lost and re-collected as seed several times since. Why hanker after such an awkward plant? One glance at Jonathan's picture (opposite) answers the question. The languorous petals drooping from the top of the stem elicit sighs from anyone who sees them. And its colour – in complete contrast to the acquiescence of its form – is deepest blood red, striking and dramatic. As the crumpled petals push off their sheltering bud cases they lengthen, shaking themselves free and stretching lower and longer to rid themselves of folds and creases, like an emerging butterfly drying its wings. The individual petals can reach 10cm/4in on nude stems usually about 30cm/1ft or occasionally taller. The only leaves form a basal clump covered in golden hairs, incidental when compared to the posy of its flowers. This is a plant that needs growing conditions which replicate its home in the damp meadows and woodland of central China – cool, moist and a little shady. It is worth any amount of effort to get it to grow, just to see its flowers even once, so many forlorn red prayer flags fluttering above a green landscape.

Everybody knows hostas. Many gardeners collect them obsessively and each year new varieties are launched – some monstrous, some tiny, some with different variegation, more puckered, smoother, with taller stems or with shorter growth. Among this multitude there are a few stars which shine brightly and the most brilliant by far is *Hosta* 'Halcyon'. Eric Smith, who bred some of the most special plants ever, was responsible for this breathtaking hosta.

He was a plantsman of vision who helped create some of the best herbaceous plants we have the privilege to grow. Among many other exceptional plants he bred and selected were extra-special varieties of *Rodgersia* (see Chapter 5), superlative bergenias in his 'composer' series and many superb hellebores.

A good gardening friend of mine, Mary Boundy, who had a beautiful garden in Tiverton, Devon, was a frequent visitor to The Plantsman Nursery which Eric Smith ran with Jim Archibald and on one trip was told about the birth of 'Halcyon'. The story goes that Eric wanted to marry two hostas which flowered at different times, envisaging that their progeny could have special qualities. He carefully put the flower of the first, ripe with pollen, in a jam jar in the small fridge in the nursery which was there mainly to keep milk for tea. When the other hosta flowered, Eric opened the jam jar and pollinated it with pollen from the first flower. Patiently he collected the seed, sowed it and grew on the resultant seedlings. The foliage of one was particularly blue with a perfect shape – ovate and tapering to a point. This is *Hosta* 'Halcyon'. His vision was rewarded with the creation of a plant classic. As it opens, each leaf is slightly rolled, with a mysterious shadow at its core. When the stems lengthen, the leaves unfurl fully, each perfectly poised in its own space. The foliage is covered with a bloom like that on grapes. If the leaves are touched, the bloom is spoiled. With most plants I am all for feeling and touching, but with this *H.* 'Halcyon'...no. We have several venerable plants which have featured on occasion in our displays at the Chelsea Flower Show. Woe betide anyone who touches their leaves in the weeks before we go to the show. Fingerprints will be examined! It is not for the judges' sake that I care about marks on the leaves, it is just that 'Halcyon' deserves to be seen in its pristine state – that is the way it is. Nothing should sully its perfect leaves.

Fritillaries have some of the most astonishingly marked and curiously coloured flowers in the plant world. *Fritillaria camschatcensis* has slaty flowers with a grape-like bloom and thrives in similar circumstances to the snakeshead fritillary. The bells of *F. persica* 'Adiyaman' are much the same colour but they throng the tall stems, contrasting exquisitely with the pointed, glaucous leaves – that is, when the plant decides to flower! Deep, rich soil and a sunny location provide the best conditions, but having supplied your bulbs with these and planted them on their sides really deep (15cm/6in is not too much) all that remains is to cross your fingers and hope for the best.

Some fritillaries need sharp drainage, gritty soil and full sun to give their all. *Fritillaria biflora* 'Martha Roderick', a diminutive beauty with delightful white bells marked with green and pink, needs special cosseting. She stands a better chance of growing well and increasing in a large clay pan or stone trough in gritty compost than ever she would in the general garden *mêlée*. The intriguing *F. verticillata* produces curious, crooked stems above its flowers with which it hooks on to nearby plants to lift itself up to its full height (37–45cm/15–18in). On the outside of its soft green bells are deeper green

Right

There is a vague air of menace about the mottled bracts and dark crimson petals of Trillium chloropetalum. *Despite its sombre colouring, it is always the centre of attention when in flower.*

lines forming a delicate tracery, while the inside is marked with maroon and green tessellations like snakeskin.

There is something of the reptile about *Trillium chloropetalum*. At first glimpse the flowers look a little dangerous and foreboding. The three horizontal bracts are darkly mottled like a lizard's back and the three central upright petals of deep crimson push forward, retract and push forward again like the heads of three hooded cobras, back to back, guarding the flower's inner sexual secrets. This magnificent show appears in the spring and, like many early birds, the trillium's flower heads stay in good shape for months because of cool weather. Added to that, most bracts last much longer than petals and continue to make an impact long after petals have disintegrated. Most years the petals are replaced by a seed head which swells inside its black coating until it bursts at the seams, exposing the large, pale seeds.

Trillium chloropetalum is an expensive plant to buy. Growing from seed is the only feasible method to increase it and seedlings can take seven long years before coming to flower. After this the performance (providing it has been found the right home) will be bigger and better each year.

Some people are fascinated by flowers the colour of dried blood or as black as coal. There are gothic gardeners who seem to prefer all their plants to be dark. They go for the blackest hellebores and love black lily turf, *Ophiopogon planiscapus* 'Nigrescens'. This is all very well when viewing plants, especially flowers, at close quarters where their rich depth of colour can be enjoyed, but, unless both background and underplanting are carefully planned, dark leaves and flowers can end up looking like so many black holes. *Trillium grandiflorum* avoids such a fate by having pure white flowers. The double form has a flurry of petals and is even more arresting. All are very desirable plants. Some, like *T. rivale*, are exquisite miniatures which need careful checks and inspections to make sure of their continued good health. In the hurly-burly of the garden they may succumb, overtaken by more boisterous individuals. It is a good idea to find them a special corner all to themselves or in company with other treasures which enjoy the same conditions.

The common name for *Melittis melissophyllum* is bastard balm. What, you might think, is a plant of such lowly birth doing here among the great and the good? But, as with many an illegitimate, there is more than a touch of the aristocrat about this interloper. I would not be without it. It loves hedgerows and woodland edges and there are steep Devonshire banks not far from Glebe Cottage that suit it very well. It is a handsome plant and, if well cultivated, makes a strong clump with upright stems clothed in slightly puckered, dark green leaves with a bit of polish about them.

The typical hooded labiate flowers of *Melittis* are borne in whorls around the stem, so from whichever angle the plant is seen some of them look the viewer right in the eye. The lower lip of the flower protrudes and the broad, central, pink stripe gives the impression of a tongue being pulled out rudely as though it could not care less what anybody thinks about its status.

Left

Potentilla x hopwoodiana *charms most people. It is the sort of plant which draws you back again and again – to examine the slightly flounced petals of such subtle colouring and to find it new partners. It makes friends easily but always wants to be the dominant player.*

Lamium orvala is devastatingly gorgeous, a must-have plant. Those seeing this dead nettle for the first time are invariably enraptured. Again, it does not thrust itself forward, but relies on its inherent grace and its dark good looks to attract admirers. Each flower consists of a deep bowl into which pollinating insects are invited via a broad landing pad, spotted and marked like the lights on a runway to guide them in. The deep green, tooth-edged leaves form a secondary roof. Both flowers and leaves are held in whorls around stout stems. When the flowers fall, the dark bracts persist and the stems retain their interest into the autumn. Happy in sun or dappled shade, it needs a good depth of soil to satisfy deep, questing roots. In sun it makes an excellent partner for *Papaver orientale* 'Patty's Plum' and will relax into the space left when the unruly poppy has been cut back to ground level. The twinkling, silvery-pink inflorescence of *Deschampsia flexuosa* employed nearby when both poppy and lamium are at their peak makes an interesting diversion, accentuating both their colour and grandeur.

In one narrow bed in the garden at Glebe Cottage *Potentilla* x *hopwoodiana* accompanies this trio. This is the queen of the tribe of potentillas and geums which make such a difference to summer beds and borders. A hybrid made almost two centuries ago between *P. recta* (bright yellow) and *P. nepalensis* (shocking pink), *P.* x *hopwoodiana* is the *crème de la crème*. Its flowers are delectable: five petals, slightly flounced, are held in a circle, their edges soft coral pink fading to cream towards the centre. Its peaches-and-cream niceness is saved from being bland by a smudge of raspberry red at the base of each petal and a dark red, velvety centre with a cluster of bronze anthers. In strong sun the colour of older flowers fades, while in the newly open flowers it is distinct, creating a wonderful variety. Annmaree Smerdon, who is such an invaluable help at Glebe Cottage Plants, dislikes the colour of the flowers vehemently. She is Australian and perhaps has no time for all that 'English Rose' complexion stuff. At first I thought she disliked it because of all the time she had to spend cleaning off old leaves from its straggly stems. On the nursery the plant is all knees and elbows, gangly and twine-toed and quite impossible to turn into a presentable individual. In the garden it assumes the most graceful poses, relaxing among other plants as though they had been put there with the sole purpose of providing a suitable background.

Further down the same bed a smattering of white from another potentilla, *P. rupestris*, lifts the planting. Its clouds of simple, white flowers mingle artlessly wherever it finds itself. When it finishes its easy-going show around midsummer, *Schizostylis coccinea* f. *alba* pirouettes into position to start a long performance that will last through to the autumn and sometimes into winter. When the flower stems start to become distinct from the surrounding sword-like foliage – a little taller and a little thicker – excitement sets in. As they lengthen and swell, the first hint of colour can be detected in the lowest buds. Soon afterwards they open fully to reveal the perfection of their mature flowers – white stars so pristine and refined they often inspire a

Right

As pristine and simple as they could be, the graceful buds and star-like flowers of Schizostylis coccinea f. alba *provide a fresh, optimistic note towards the end of summer's flagging pageant.*

cutting-back of nearby spent flowers and untidy foliage to supply more salubrious surroundings.

Schizostylis are from South Africa and it is often assumed that South African plants adore hot, dry sites. Christopher Lloyd once remonstrated with me for including *Kniphofia natalensis* on the corner of my Chelsea Flower Show display reserved for plants which loved dry conditions. He pointed out that *Kniphofia* need damp soil and often occur in marshy grassland in their homeland. *Schizostylis* also need moist conditions and thrive in fertile soil. Their performance after a dry spring and summer is poor. Where conditions suit, they will make lush clumps with strong stems bearing substantial flowers. It is said that they will grow in shallow water. We have never tried this but to keep up flower quality we divide and replant yearly with plenty of added humus.

The individual flowers of *Schizostylis coccinea* f. *alba* open in succession from long, graceful buds. They are starry and elegant with a touch of green in the throat. The style, as their Latin name denotes, is split and the anthers dangle at the end of three separate stamens. The anthers are thick with cream pollen which makes the flowers look even whiter, like an advert for soap powder. *Schizostylis coccinea* 'Major' is a much more imposing plant. Its rich red flowers with more rounded petals than the white form make it very showy.

We have several large clumps of *Agapanthus*. Some are named varieties, others hybrids which Richard Lee made at Rosemoor in Devon, using named Headbourne Hybrids. *Agapanthus* are a promiscuous lot. Some of their offspring are worthy of a special place, others are indifferent. At their best they are gracious plants with spheres of flower. Apart from a tiny minority of white-flowered forms, all are blue. The blue can vary though from the palest, as in *A.* 'Silver Mist' with flowers the colour of a new dawn, to the deepest, darkest inky-blue, as in *A.* 'Midnight'. Stature varies, too, from tiny to majestic.

For gardeners who have no time to move plants backwards and forwards to spend a winter sojourn under cover, the deciduous forms of *Agapanthus* are the hardiest. Many of these have smaller flowers but produce them prolifically. A good clump can make twenty stems of delightful, blue drumsticks after just a few seasons. The seed heads are also ornamental. The seeds themselves are intriguing – like nothing so much as tiny tadpoles with the plump seed attached to a see-through, black tail. They are easy to grow, preferably sown fresh and pricked out individually the next spring. With a bit of luck they should come to flower the following season when the wheat can be sorted from the chaff.

It is always interesting to hear how differently people describe plants. In the case of *Gladiolus papilio* Purpureoauratus Group, everyone seems to be turned on by the same three factors: the subtle colour – dirty-mauve and dusty-yellow – strange markings, with the lower petals replicating the patterns on a butterfly's wings, and the mysterious flower structure, with the upper petals forming a hood or roof over the flower's cavernous interior.

*Mysterious and slightly
aloof, the hooded flowers
of* Gladiolus papilio
*Purpureoauratus Group
are elegance personified;
a far cry from the stiff-
stemmed, gaudy, florists'
gladioli. How can such a
subtle flower attract so
much attention?*

Gladiolus belong to the same Iridaceae family as *Schizostylis*. In bud
Gladiolus papilio Purpureoauratus Group bears a striking similarity, but
as the *Gladiolus* buds open it is clear that they contain something very
different. Almost every visitor who sees them in our garden at Glebe Cottage
begs an introduction if they have not met the plant before.

All *Gladiolus papilio* Purpureoauratus Group needs to perform is a sun-
baked spot. On light soils it will increase at a rate of knots; on heavier soils
it is more reticent. This is not a *Gladiolus* out of the Dame Edna Everage
stable. There is nothing over the top about it. From its graceful 90cm/3ft
flower stems to the slender swords of its glaucous foliage, it is a picture
of understated elegance.

Tricyrtis or toad lilies, so called because of their darkly spotted and
splodged flowers, have a quiet but intriguing beauty. Seeing *T. formosana*
Stolonifera Group for the first time is thrilling, but even gardeners who have
known it for years are still stopped in their tracks when the first flowers open
each autumn. Who could be blasé about such an elegant and individual
plant? Dark stems are clothed with dark green, oval leaves topped with
mysterious flowers, their faces uplifted revealing an intricate arrangement
of stigma and anthers. This gorgeous oriental spreads its roots just beneath
the surface of the soil. It loves woodland conditions and prefers a cool root
run, so a thick mulch of leaf mould always helps to retain moisture and
improve performance.

Most *Polemonium* are a bit on the prosaic side. Jacob's ladder, *P. caeruleum,*
is a good plant for beginners. Its prolific self-seeding and ease of culture
encouraged me enormously when I first started gardening; but it is a stiff
plant and once the flowers have fallen (about a fortnight after they first open),
there is not a great deal to anticipate. There are exceptions to every rule.
One or two Jacob's ladders are in the first flight of herbaceous plants. They
are mainly hybrids between *P. caeruleum, P. carneum* and *P. reptans* and most
of them are sterile, producing no seed of their own. Their sterility has two
obvious consequences. Vegetative propagation by cuttings or division (or
possibly by micro-propagation) is the only way to increase them, but their
inability to set seed is a huge advantage as far as their performance in the
garden goes. When most plants have successfully set seed, there is no need
to carry on flowering. Although a few plants prolong their flowering season
as an insurance policy, most peter out as seed is set. Gardeners deadhead
flowers not just to tidy up but also to prevent seed being set and to encourage
the production of further flowers as the plant tries to fulfil its *raison d'être* –
reproduction. If a plant is sterile there is no reason for it to stop flowering and
it is liable to give a long performance.

Polemonium 'Bressingham Purple' inherits the glorious rich blue flowers
of *P. caeruleum*. Its foliage is deep maroon and, after a spell of cold weather,
can be almost black. The major drawback with Jacob's ladders is that they
are susceptible to mildew, especially when they are dry at their roots for a

Preceding pages
Tricyrtis formosana
*Stolonifera Group looks
exotic and difficult,
but is easy to cultivate
given humus-rich soil
and shade.*
Opposite
Polemonium carneum
*makes a branching plant
with simple flowers in
open clusters, changing in
colour from delicate peach
to lavender.*

prolonged period. The problem is exacerbated if their top-growth is damp through peremptory watering or brief showers. Planting with plenty of moisture-retaining organic matter and mulching with the same material plus thorough watering in prolonged dry spells can prevent it. The darker the foliage, the more disfiguring is the effect of the mildew.

The foliage of *Polemonium* 'Lambrook Mauve' never seems to succumb to mildew. It has a bronze cast which enhances the round-petalled flowers of soft lavender, produced from mid-spring to late summer. When the flowers fall the calyces which remain have ornamental value in their own right. Lavender flowers are hard to place. Put them next to anything remotely crimson or red and they look washed-out. Against blue they look mucky. But with yellow they can be themselves. Next to the vivid chrome yellow of doronicums or the pale lemon of primroses, their flower colour is enhanced. The flowers of *P. carneum* make partnerships much more easily than those of *P.* 'Lambrook Mauve' because their own flower colour contains a whole range of nuances. Individual flowers within each flower head change from peach to palest lilac as they age. They are lit by anthers drenched in orange pollen.

Polemonium 'Glebe Cottage Lilac' was a gift from our garden. Its foliage is bright green and its flowers soft lavender. It makes a tall, branching plant, in flower for three months. One of its most enchanting qualities is the way in which the flower colour fades, so that there is a range of colour within one head. Although sterile, it produces rich orange-yellow pollen which further enhances the flower colour. Its clustered flowers consort perfectly with the bobbing heads of *Aquilegia longissima*.

Aquilegia longissima is one of the most exquisite flowers in the world. Its petals are a pale, soft, buttery-yellow. Of a deeper yellow, its spurs, sometimes up to 15cm/6in long, are swept elegantly backwards, giving the whole flower the look of a ship's figurehead or a classic heroine with the wind blowing through her blond hair.

Like so many of the most desirable aquilegias, *A. longissima* hails from the New World where it grows in the mountains of the southernmost States right down to Mexico. Several American species, including *A. longissima*, its close cousin *A. chrysantha*, *A. formosa*, with dainty, red and yellow flowers, and *A. coerulea*, have been hybridized to give birth to the familiar, long-spurred hybrids. Seed strains such as *A.* 'Dragonfly' and *A.* McKana Group give us varieties with a wealth of multi-coloured, long-spurred flowers.

It seems strange that two birds as different as the eagle (*aquila*) and the dove (*columbus*) should give their names to the same flower. The petals supposedly resemble the outspread wings of either bird and the spurs their arched necks and heads. Whether aquilegia or columbine, this genus offers us some of the most garden-worthy and decorative of plants. All have wonderful foliage which emerges early, creating tuffets of bright green among the sharp verticals of daffodils and other vernal bulbs. They are among the most telling of springtime plants for both foliage and flowers.

Many of the North American species are short-lived but can be grown easily from seed. Most of the species come true from seed if they are isolated from others, but the whole family has a reputation for promiscuity and even incest! In gardens where *Aquilegia vulgaris*, a European species, dominates, countless forms of varying colour and shape can occur. It is these self-made, cottage-garden hybrids which inspire the common name of grannies' bonnets. One of the oldest forms is *A. v.* var. *stellata* 'Nora Barlow', named after Charles Darwin's daughter but recorded much earlier as 'The Rose Columbine' in the seventeenth century. Its thickly clustered petals are soft pink, green and white.

Only a few Far Eastern aquilegias are in general cultivation. One of them has the bonus of unexpected but particularly delectable perfume. If it had no scent, it might easily be overlooked. *Aquilegia viridiflora* is small and dainty with numerous nodding flowers of chocolate brown and mossy green suspended from fine stems like fairy lanterns in an enchanted wood. The flowers hang gracefully, their spurs aloft turned neatly inward and a collection of overlapping anthers coyly peeping from the bronze skirts. Its foliage too is exquisite, glaucous, neat and much divided. It is best grown in an elevated position, a raised bed or container or even individually in a pot where its perfume and subtle demeanour can be enjoyed at close quarters.

A close view of *Digitalis parviflora* yields a wealth of fascinating insights. This distinctive foxglove works on so many different levels in the garden, it would be difficult to overstate its versatility. In its first year rosettes of elongated, dark green leaves lie flat on the ground. They are tough and shiny, etched with linear veins which emphasize their length. In their second year,

Left

Digitalis parviflora *has real charisma. It is fascinating in close-up and from a distance; whether in flower or seed, its close-packed spikes make emphatic focal points.*

at the onset of summer, slender, pale green columns emerge, rising rapidly as straight as a die. As they rocket upwards, the flower buds become distinct. They lengthen and turn outwards, simultaneously changing colour until the whole spike is thick with bronze bells. Look down the spike from above and the flowers form a spiral. The magical geometry of growth which exists in all plants is laid bare. In close-up its flowers have a wealth of detail – tiny, intricate patterns mark the interior of its narrow bells which are covered inside and out with fine fluff. Two 'headlight' anthers full of yellow pollen are poised either side of the entrance to anoint insects with their riches.

Foxgloves are usually associated with shady conditions. Though it frequents woodland edges in its native southern Europe, *Digitalis parviflora* is perfectly at home in more northerly gardens, basking in a sunny spot. Its 90cm/3ft pillars are ideal as an architectural end-piece to a tapering border in a hot, dry position. Mixed with achilleas and soft grasses, its obelisks provide a series of focal points to guide the eye through a naturalistic planting. Later on its tapering spires take on an even more striking structural significance as the fabulously furry flowers fall and polished, barbed seed heads take their place, packed tightly together in bronze ramrods. The seed heads may stand, sentinel-like, throughout the winter.

Most seductive sophisticates are at their best during 'prime time' – early summer to mid-autumn – but hellebores have something to offer for even longer and provide voluptuous beauty at the time of year we need it most, yet least expect to find it. *Helleborus* x *hybridus* is not herbaceous. Unless we remove the big, shiny, palmate leaves for reasons of hygiene or tidiness, it will continuously produce leaves, so that there will be something to see even on the bleakest winter's day. Flowering starts early and the big Lenten roses are unfazed even by fierce cold. After a heavy frost the flower stalks can be levelled to the ground, their precious blossoms frozen to the earth. If the day warms up sufficiently, the limp stems will miraculously recover.

On our nursery we grow lots of hellebores and frequently take them to early flower shows 320km/200 miles away at the Royal Horticultural Society in London. Daylight is in short supply when we exhibit at these shows and our van must be packed the day before departure. There is always the chance of a severe frost and, with the metal body of the van turning it into a big refrigerator, steps must be taken to protect the precious cargo. We usually ask our kind neighbours who run a dairy herd if we can keep the packed van overnight in their cow shed where the temperature never drops too low, thanks to all those warm bodies. Since we leave early, as milking starts, nobody is inconvenienced.

One of the most entertaining sights at these flower shows is to watch gardeners of every description, and presumably with all sorts of gardens, select their hellebores. As in some unique dating agency, complex manoeuvres of inspection, rejection and further inspection continue until the happy pair is united. There are cases of bigamy and occasionally polyandry. The worst

Left

Nowadays Helleborus x
hybridus *are sold as seed
strains rather than named
varieties. Every seedling is
unique, so we can all
choose our very own.*

culprits for acquiring a harem are almost invariably women. Beware buying a hellebore for someone else. It is a bit like arranging a blind date.

Hellebores are difficult to divide, so few plants can be propagated from any one parent. They take ages to settle in and re-establish a flowering routine – so all in all selling named cultivars is doomed to failure. Sadly, over-division has led to the demise of some exceptional plants. On the other hand many of the named or selected plants from the pioneering hybridizing of Helen Ballard and Elizabeth Strangman have formed the backbone for seed strains developed by nurseries on both sides of the Atlantic.

Most hellebores hang their heads to protect their pollen from driving rain. Some hybridists of *Helleborus* x *hybridus* seek to 'rectify' this by attempting to breed plants whose flowers look upwards. But there is magic in turning up the flowers to investigate their hidden secrets. The spots and markings can be fascinating and the stamens, anthers and nectaries clustered around the style and stigma form intriguing centres. These nectaries are modified petals designed to attract solitary bees which are so scarce at flowering time and yet so essential to the pollination process. The 'petals' are in fact sepals, which usually form the outer protective casing of a bud and its flower. In hellebores they still do this, but also become petals. In nature they are usually green and occasionally white, pink, purple or yellow.

Nowadays the best hellebores are produced as seed strains rather than named varieties. Each generation has the potential to outdo the last as selection of parent plants becomes more and more exacting. The process of pollination is a simple craft. The business of selection, having an eye for a plant, is an art. Because it takes at least three years between the initial pollination and the manifestation of its results in the form of a flowering plant, it is worthwhile spending some time selecting parents. According to my heroine, Elizabeth Strangman, you should choose the mother plant for strong growth and for the shape of its flowers. (I love rounded flowers with rounded petals best.) The father, the pollen donor, will contribute to colour and shape and, perhaps, esoteric characteristics like very large flowers.

If you have no hellebores fit for procreation, buy two good plants in pots with a few buds each. Pollination can then take place under cover, a much more attractive proposition in early spring than sex in the garden. Limit your efforts to one or two crosses. It is tempting to cross everything in sight, but once you have done the deed you are committed to rearing the results or committing mass infanticide.

As distinct individuals with unique personalities, hellebores manifest the beauty that sets seductive sophisticates in a class of their own.

7.

Dainty
& detailed

Left

Getting up close to
Veronica gentianoides
reveals a wealth of
unimagined detail.
This is a lovely garden-
worthy plant with
slender spires of cool
blue speedwell flowers.

There are so many levels at which plants can be enjoyed: in the abstract as components of a design; as individual juxtapositions of flower, stem and leaf with their own distinctive personalities; and in microcosm in the perfection of their detail. Eye-to-eye views are a revelation. To observe plants at close quarters opens up new layers of appreciation. One of the delights of hands-on gardening is the confidential insight it allows into the detail of plants. On hands and knees is the best way to appreciate the structure of a corydalis with its lark's toe flowers balancing on hair-fine stems. At ground level the symmetry of unfurling fern fronds can be viewed intimately and the mathematical beauty of their construction savoured at first hand.

ONE OF MY BEST GARDENING friends ever, Sonia Roffey, introduced me to *Veronica gentianoides* early in my gardening days. She told me how useful it was – an evergreen speedwell which would grow happily in shade – but what she stressed was its simple beauty. I have used *V. gentianoides* on numerous occasions, both in the garden and as a constituent in our Chelsea Flower Show displays. Despite this close acquaintance, it was not until I scrutinized a flower which had fallen from the plant that I realized how intricate are its markings and saw the way in which the blue lines, which form a tracery across the petals' surface, converge to create a concentrated blue centre.

Looking at *Veronica gentianoides* through the lens of Jonathan's camera was even more revealing. The flower spikes rise as narrow columns from the centre of its lush, dark green rosettes, with the buds tightly packed against the stem. At this stage, and as the buds begin to open, the green of the stems mixes with the pale blue of the flowers to make the flower spikes seem turquoise, a soft sea colour. The flowers soon open their blue eyes, looking straight out from the stems. In common with all speedwells, *V. gentianoides* does not hang on to its individual flowers for very long. The fallen flowers make a carpet of confetti across the clumps. As the flowers fall from the base of the spike, it lengthens. Eventually a host of green pillars remains with a few flowers left at the top. Those obsessed with gardening as a form of housework would chop them off at this stage. More laid-back gardeners appreciate the counterpoint between the lush, viridian, horizontal carpet made by the basal rosettes and the slender verticals of the flower spikes which persist for ages. Plants, like people, often have much to commend them when they are 'going over'.

Some *Epimedium*, on the other hand, seem to have discovered the secret of eternal youth. Several robust varieties have evergreen foliage which admirably furnishes the difficult ground around deciduous trees. (It would probably persist forever were the gardener not to intervene.) The burnished midwinter foliage of *E.* x *versicolor* 'Neosulphureum' is a sight for sore eyes. As the weather gets colder, the leaves become more and more bronze and their beauty is given an extra shine by relentless winter rain. Left to themselves, evergreen epimediums would get taller and taller as new spring growth is forced to push itself through older foliage. Flowers too would become attenuated, struggling through the undergrowth to see the light of day. In the garden, best practice is to get in with the shears, cutting to 5cm/2in above ground level just when the new growth is visible as it pushes determinedly through around the bases of the older leaf stems. Leave it any longer and shears will need to be exchanged for nail scissors to avoid decapitating the new growth.

Most years this haircut means forgoing what is still a fine display. But the beauty which unfolds soon afterwards is so entrancing we forget about what was. Slender, new leaves of soft donkey brown accompany the daintiest of pale yellow flowers in the first dance of the season. Stems lengthen, flowers and leaves stretch and open, composing themselves into a perfect *pas de deux*.

Right
Like some extra-terrestrial insect, the flowers of Epimedium grandiflorum *'Nanum Freya' hover on wiry stems above the purple-edged leaves, spurs outstretched. Some epimediums have even longer spurs. All deserve to be studied at close quarters.*

Left

Like most umbellifers,
Chaerophyllum hirsutum
*'Roseum' has flowers
within flowers that are
held on individual stems
which extend as the
flowers unfurl. As each
small bouquet opens to
display petals, stamens
and anthers, the whole
look of the plant changes.*

The quality of these new leaves is exquisite. They are so tender as to be almost translucent. The spidery-fine flowers look just as fragile. In fact both are tremendously tough; like the best of ballet dancers they have strength and resilience underlying their poise and grace.

The beautiful and floriferous cultivars of *Epimedium grandiflorum* from Japan appreciate 'woodsy' conditions too. They lose their leaves during winter but the spring foliage of some varieties is exquisite. *Epimedium grandiflorum* f. *violaceum* and many of its cultivars have smoky-purple young leaves. Both stems and leaf margins of *E. g.* 'Nanum Freya' are dark blackcurrant. The deep violet crimson flowers are highlighted by four white-spurred petals which, although initially tucked into the buds, become a prominent feature when the flower opens. The diminutive, fresh green leaves of *E. g.* 'Nanum' are outlined in red, a foil for its exquisite white flowers, scattered like snowflakes over the foliage. From naturalistic woodland planting to creating a special cameo in a small urban garden, epimediums are the most versatile of shade-loving plants. The fairy charm of their flowers and their handsome foliage bring the dreariest corners to life.

Some umbellifers have intricately detailed flowers. They can be seen on many levels, becoming increasingly more complex as our eyes move in – like a selection of frames from a movie, they yield different realities within the same head of flower. From a distance *Anthriscus sylvestris*, cow-parsley or Queen Anne's lace, makes a fine, frothy picture, full of creamy softness. Closer up, with the whole flower head in frame, we are aware of its structure, of the individual stems all emanating in a starburst from the summit of the main stem and each supporting its own smaller umbel of flowers. We can move closer again to study each perfect flower. Such a feast for the eyes – and all for free.

Few of us have room for cow-parsley in our gardens – it spreads too fast and too furiously. But we can accommodate a plant or two of *Chaerophyllum hirsutum* 'Roseum', which is a plant of great gentility. It understates its own case, with a quiet harmony of soft lilac pink flowers, matt, mid-green leaves and brown stems. Like an unassuming person, hardly noticed at first, its charm becomes more and more apparent at each subsequent meeting. Even its first emergence is reticent. The leaves are almost sessile and the embryonic flowers, clutched by their stems, lie flat against the dark ground. Plants in pots behave in exactly the same way. Customers in the nursery who are not acquainted with the plant look at one pot after another, determined to find one which does not look as though it has been trampled. In its own time it sorts itself out and within weeks of appearing is well on the way to making a big, beautifully branching plant. As each episode of its quiet drama unfolds, there is more and more to wonder at. It reaches a perfection of detail when its first umbels are fully opened with the extra decoration of tiny stigma and stamens.

Selinum wallichianum combines strength and structure with delicate refinement. In spring it rises later than most perennials but, once it has

Right

The beautifully constructed, lacy flowers of Orlaya grandiflora *lighten up ponderous plantings. The ring of extra petals flags the message to passing insects that there are sweet treats within.*

decided to get up, it briskly spreads out its basal leaves to form a neat mat. Each leaf is intricately divided, making big, deep green doilies among clumps of flowering daffodils or the fresh, new foliage of daylilies or phlox. Strong, ribbed stems start to push up, endowed with more fretted leaves making layer upon lacy layer. The stems branch but the tiered effect is maintained. During late summer the stems part and the flower buds begin to emerge. They are inverted and swaddled by the pinky-bronze stems like flamingos or swans with their heads tucked under their wings. On emerging, the flower stems begin to straighten and extend until the fat buds, swathed by long, white bracteoles, are held horizontally. The bracteoles, having protected the embryonic buds, part and fold outwards until they are completely inverted, making little skirts around the stems. By this time the pure white struts which support the individual clusters of flowers are well on their way to separating. Each flower head becomes a plateau composed of tens of smaller florets which in turn are made up of myriad tiny flowers. The arrangement of the slender stems which form the scaffolding supporting the floor of the flowers is miraculous. Each one is exactly the right length to hold its own load. The flower heads are impeccably fashioned, their plates perfect circles composed of smaller circles.

Viewed in sharp focus, *Selinum wallichianum* is a fascinating collection of interrelated parts. It lends itself more to time-lapse photography than to descriptions in words.

In *Orlaya grandiflora* each umbel is enhanced by a ruff of larger, sterile florets formed in much the same manner as those of a lacecap hydrangea or *Viburnum plicatum* 'Mariesii'. Although a biennial, it is a must for any well-clothed garden, providing lacy touches around plainer, more austere plants. Its frilliness is never over-the-top, though. There is perfection in the form of both the whole plant and the heads of flower. It is best grown on in pots and planted out individually when its rosettes of finely cut leaves (like those of chervil but even prettier) are fully extended, but before the crooked flower stems emerge and straighten.

One of my most abiding memories is coming across colonies of *Cyclamen hederifolium* growing in the boles of beech trees in the Abruzzi mountains outside Rome. It was early September and they were at the beginning of their flowering season. The immensity of the trees emphasized the fragility of the cyclamen's tiny pink flowers. At close quarters, they are intriguing at every stage. The scrolled buds are long and narrow. As the petals gradually unfurl they draw backwards as though surprised to find themselves upside down.

Nature is always ingenious and nowhere more so than in the distribution of cyclamen seeds. As the flowers fade after pollination, their stems curl up, spiralling down until they reach ground level. The seed case expands gently, protected by the emerging leaves. Eventually it splits and the seeds are exposed. Each one is a tiny tuber. Meanwhile their starchy coating has changed to sugar, attracting ants which move in and carry them away, thus

Left

*Soliloquies in the mud.
The dainty propeller
flowers of* Cyclamen
coum *subsp.* coum
f. coum *(Pewter Group)
'Maurice Dryden' need
to be studied at close hand.
They appear simultaneously
with the shiny, orbicular
leaves in midwinter,
lasting for weeks.*

ensuring that young plants are not so close as to compete with their parents. Sometimes the seeds are carried even further afield by wasps, also attracted to the sugar. As flowers fade, leaves begin to appear.

There are few plants which offer both such exquisite flowers and such ornately decorative foliage as the ivy-leaved cyclamen, *C. hederifolium*. Every plant has unique markings and, like human fingerprints, no two are ever the same. A mass planting in the late autumn or winter is more fascinating than the most intricately detailed Persian carpet.

In late winter *Cyclamen hederifolium* are joined by the foliage and flowers of *C. coum*, which in its typical form has round, leathery, dark green leaves with the same intriguing propeller formation. The usual flower colour is vivid magenta. Seedlings can be pale pink and occasionally white, but even the white-flowered varieties are stained with pink at the base of their petals. At one time *C. coum* was described as always having plain green leaves and varieties with silver markings were classed as a separate species – *C. orbiculatum*. Now bulb firms list distinct, silver-leaved and silver-marked varieties as forms of *C. coum*.

Several varieties of *Corydalis* are worth studying at close quarters. *C. flexuosa* grows in the wild with *Epimedium davidii*. In a garden setting too, the soft blue and warm yellow of their respective flowers make a beautiful combination. The spreading, succulent growth and bronze, ferny leaves of the *Corydalis* complement the shiny, green, pinnate leaves of the *Epimedium*, extending interest when the two are out of flower. The first time I saw *Corydalis flexuosa* was not on some Chinese woodland floor but on a large trolley being pulled by two men in brown warehouseman's coats. It was travelling past the stand at the Royal Horticultural Society where I was wrestling with a large tree stump and a quantity of spring plants. One of the men was tall – Martyn Rix – one shorter – John D'Arcy. They are the R&D of the plant-hunting trio CD&R. The third member of this illustrious group is Jamie Compton. Their initials together with collection numbers appear at the end of the names of a host of good plants. At the time in question they were putting on a display of some of the plants they had collected on a plant-hunting expedition in West Sichuan. There were epimediums, sanicles, ferns and tiarellas, but without doubt the star of the show was *C. flexuosa* in three distinct varieties. Their beautiful display was awash with it and crowds flocked to see this wondrous plant for the first time. Since then, many thousands of gardeners have made its acquaintance.

Corydalis flexuosa 'Père David' is the best all-rounder, spreading well from stolons with mid-blue flowers and green foliage. *Corydalis flexuosa* 'China Blue' is my favourite for its other-worldly, almost turquoise flowers and olive green foliage. It is taller, too, but more circumspect, spreading slowly. It is huge fun to combine *C. f.* 'Purple Leaf' with other plants. Because of its coppery foliage and the soft lilac mixed in with the blue of its flowers, the combinations in which it can participate are legion. The three varieties

Preceding pages
Corydalis flexuosa
*'Purple Leaf', with
coppery foliage, is one of
several selections with
blue 'lark's-spur' flowers.*
Opposite
Francoa ramosa *has the
endearing habit of
opening all the flowers
along its slender spikes at
the same time.*

introduced by CD&R are quite distinctive individuals, but beware: if they are to be kept that way, seedlings must be plucked or seed heads removed. They will interbreed at the drop of a hat and, if precautions are not taken, will soon become indistinguishable. In the USA *C. f.* 'Blue Panda', introduced by Reuben Hatch before the CD&R plants, is a favourite. All these plants will bloom incessantly from early summer until autumn, provided they do not dry out.

Nepeta govaniana is the only catmint with a dainty personality and is an exception in more ways than one. Its flower is unique among nepetas: creamy-yellow, tiny and more widely spaced than usual. These flowers dance on elegant, branching stems above softly felted, bright lime green leaves. Catmints smell, but not like this. The whole plant is aromatic. It hails from the Himalayas where it grows in damp, slightly acid soil on woodland margins quite unlike the conditions favoured by most catmints. Not only does it prefer more moisture than its relatives, but it loves cool and is happiest in dappled shade. *Nepeta govaniana* is one of those quiet, self-effacing plants which nonetheless everyone notices and, having seen, must immediately dash out and plant. Once you have it, you wonder how you could have managed without it.

There could be no other place for bridal wreath, *Francoa ramosa*. Each flower is small and perfect with four rounded petals and a dimpled centre. Clustered evenly around the top 15cm/6in of the stem, the flowers are individually dainty and also have impact *en masse*. The bold, basal rosettes are evergreen, bright green in the white- and palest-flowered forms. The leaves of plants with darker flowers are often dark and polished and in cold weather assume an even more burnished look. The darker the leaves and flowers, the hardier the plant.

Francoa sonchifolia Rogerson's form, one of the toughest, has exceptionally dark, shiny foliage emblazoned with occasional patches of crimson. The deep pink buds open to even deeper pink, almost magenta flowers and are of good size and quality on strong stems. It must be propagated by removing some of the outside rosettes, stripping their bottom leaves and pushing them into well-drained, gritty compost. The fibrous roots are a clue to the sort of situation it prefers – woodsy and moist with plenty of humus. It is closely related to saxifrages and heucheras.

Looking in close up at the intricacies and minute detail within plants gives us a fresh take on their individuality. The intimacy offered by this bee's eye view reveals a wealth of features not noticeable in the usual context of the relationship between gardener and plant.

8.

Gatecrashers

Left

Two infamous interlopers with the same growth habit: soft lavender Verbena bonariensis *and sharp yellow* Patrinia scabiosifolia. *Although both often turn up without an invitation, they are usually made welcome, especially when they arrive together.*

There are some plants at the garden party who were never asked. Many are weeds deposited by birds or parachuted in on the breeze, which we spend hours removing, trying to ensure they will not spill their progeny into our flowerbeds. But not all gatecrashers are unwelcome guests. Some we welcome with open arms into any venue from tiny urban plot to vast rural estate. By definition, they are self-seeders. Many are annuals or biennials. Others are perennials, brought by seed wiped from a blackbird's beak, caught in fur or feather or jettisoned from a flowerbed yards away and now appearing magically in the crook of a wall or the space between flags. However they arrive, nobody asks to see their invitation. Purists can easily remove them should they have the temerity to interfere with grand designs. The rest of us think ourselves lucky and make the most of the gatecrashers' spontaneity.

141

TIME AND TIME AGAIN, WHEN ASKED about a winning combination, gardeners have to admit they had nothing to do with it. 'It just put itself there,' they marvel. Occasionally gatecrashers create a cameo but generally they throw themselves around in gay abandon with the profligacy of cornfield weeds (before the introduction of herbicides). *Arum italicum* subsp. *italicum* 'Marmoratum', brought by birds, is one of the most useful plants imaginable during the dire winter months. Tightly scrolled leaves thrust their way through the cooling soil just as the majority of herbaceous plants are retiring for their winter hibernation. These great, glossy, green arrowheads, ribbed and veined starkly in white, appear in quick succession until there is a great sheaf of them. They may arrive in a rush, but they have tremendous staying power, remaining in pristine condition throughout the worst vagaries of the winter and hosting, in late spring, a series of pale green 'cuckoo-pint' flowers, barely discernible among the statuesque leaves. Throughout the summer months they are out of sight and out of mind. Suddenly, as autumn takes over, the stems of berries come rocketing through bare soil. Glistening green on emerging, they soon change through orange to brightest, polished red. Poisonous to humans, the seeds are manna for hungry birds who soon destroy their perfect symmetry. Although it is annoying when stems are stripped bare, there is always the promise of new plants as compensation.

 Arum italicum subsp. *italicum* 'Marmoratum' may appear anywhere. A happy combination is created when they pop up alongside the see-through seed heads of honesty, *Lunaria annua*. In cultivation for centuries, honesty or money plant is still a feature of many gardens. Although a biennial, each

Right

Arum italicum *subsp.*
italicum *'Marmoratum'*
has a dual personality.
Some gardeners cherish
it for its marbled leaves,
others for its stems of
bright red berries (seen
here growing through
Stachys byzantina
'Cotton Boll'). Most of us
value both foliage and
berries – wherever they
crop up.

plant living only two years, once it has established a base-camp, it can go on forever, sowing itself with abandon to become a permanent feature, a treat to anticipate every spring. In country venues it often leaves the confines of the garden and makes itself at home on banks and verges, its deep purply-pink flowers amalgamating joyously with the vivid lime green bracts of wood spurge. When seed is set, it makes its escape on silver wheels, the paper-thin discs blown and rolled this way and that until they lodge in some unremitting corner, the end of their journey. Gradually weather turns the discs to skeletons; their precious passengers are gently lowered to earth to start a new colony.

When honesty heads are caught suddenly in a shaft of light from the low sun, they can be transformed momentarily into glistening moons in orbit around their parchment stems. The seed heads of *Lunaria annua* 'Alba Variegata' are just as exciting in the spotlight, but have creamy-white, variegated leaves and pure white flowers. This is an aristocratic honesty although indistinguishable from a commoner in its first year, its foliage rough and dark green like all the others. It is only in its flowering year that it shows its true colours and demonstrates its noble birth.

Verbena bonariensis has become an essential ingredient in naturalistic plantings. Its informal, branching habit of growth is exactly *comme il faut*. But its greatest value in wild schemes is its ability to self-seed prolifically. As it wends its merry way it helps integrate even quite disparate plants into a cohesive whole. Should its colonizing ambitions get out of hand, and the look become too samey, it can easily be pulled up. These casualties of overcrowding can be transplanted, any long stems cut back before replanting. They do not transplant well, though, and growing from seed is a better option.

Patrinia scabiosifolia shares the same habit of growth with *Verbena bonariensis* although it is unrelated, belonging to the valerian family. Their similarity can be exploited to dramatic effect by planting them side by side, preferably in swathes, to mingle with each other. Although their form is almost identical, their colour is opposite though harmonious. The soft lavender of the verbena mixes perfectly with the sharp, citric yellow of the patrinia. Even when the patrinia flowers have fallen they leave behind lime-green calyces which last for months. When the two get going there is nothing to beat them. *Patrinia scabiosifolia* will self-seed efficiently, although in a cold, wet summer seed may not set properly.

There is one plant which is particularly famous for its ability to crop up in unexpected places. *Eryngium giganteum* is more often known as Miss Wilmott's Ghost. Nowadays it is a familiar plant. Familiar, but not friendly. It is a big biennial sea holly, which in its second year throws up 90cm/3ft stems with great, silvery-bracted flowers. The bracts are armed with some of the most malicious spikes around. Ellen Wilmott was a wealthy and influential gardener with several gardens and a host of gardeners. She was a woman with definite sensibilities and, by all accounts, believed that others should share them. From time to time, she was prevailed upon to look at

other people's gardens. If she suspected they might be a teeny bit dull, she would pack her pockets with seed from *E. giganteum* and as she walked around would broadcast it in the particularly boring bits. The next year up would come large, green rosettes and, the year after, astonished garden owners would be greeted by a jungle of sharp, silvery flowers. Once Miss Wilmott's Ghost has seeded in a garden, it is impossible to eradicate. The haunting continues.

Poppies are just as persistent. Poppy seed can live for hundreds of years. Germination often follows the ground being disturbed. *Papaver rhoeas*, the corn poppy, is a nice illustration, a new generation germinating each year as the land was ploughed and the grain scattered. *Papaver somniferum*, the opium poppy, is a crop itself in some parts of the world. In our gardens it is appreciated for its ornamental value. At a rapid (some would say alarming) pace its stout stems zoom up, wrapped with wavy-edged, glaucous leaves and lateral shoots all terminating in plump, dimpled buds. At this stage there are waves of excitement to see what colour and form the flowers will have when the buds finally burst. Even when there is only one poppy in the garden, its progeny can be completely different from one another and from their mother. There are reds, pinks and purples, black and white. Some are single and elegant, some as fussy and frilly as a Barbara Cartland blouse. All are followed by pepper-pot seed pods, which are immensely decorative in their own right.

Sometimes we sow poppies deliberately if we are hankering after a particular colour to wash through a border. Seed firms often sell selected varieties, though inevitably there are plenty of rogues! I love this riotous invasion whether it is planned or spontaneous.

It is easy to pull up poppies if they do not fit our plans but there are other incursions which are much more difficult to curb. So far our gatecrashers are all short-lived self-seeders but other uninvited guests may stay indefinitely. Once rosebay willow-herb, *Chamerion angustifolium* (formerly *Epilobium angustifolium*), has turned up, nothing will persuade it to go home. Such a nomadic beast probably has no home to go to. It is such a beauty, especially pure white *C. a.* 'Album' and the soft pink 'Stahl Rose', that many of us are tempted to plant it. The flower stems are tall, up to 1.2m/4ft if it is growing well, and because it seems to enjoy rude good health, there is usually a host of them.

Chamerion angustifolium occurs in the wild in Europe, America and Asia. It has such an invasive habit it is easy to imagine its thrusting white roots making the transatlantic journey under the sea and crossing Alps and Himalayas with consummate ease. No doubt it will turn up in the Antipodes. Planted in buckets or other impregnable containers, sunk in beds or borders, it can be enjoyed without fear of imminent invasion… except what are those green shoots thrusting up on the other side of the path?

Sometimes it is the unexpected guest who brings to the party just what was lacking.

9.

Drama queens

Left
A riotous assembly of drama queens vies for attention in Christopher Lloyd's Exotic Garden at Great Dixter, East Sussex.

Some plants cannot be ignored. Try as we might to concentrate on the exquisite detail of an intricate leaf or to appreciate the subtleties of a delicate colour combination, our eyes are drawn relentlessly to plants which demand undivided attention, and demand it now. It could be a plant's stature – the soaring spikes of foxtail lilies, thrusting red hot pokers or the enormous umbrellas of *Gunnera manicata* – that stops you in your tracks. It may be colour which attracts – the garden equivalent of strobe lighting – as in retina-searing red crocosmia, made all the redder by green leaves of an identical tone. You can hardly bear it, but you just can't look away. Most of these sumptuous exhibitionists reach the height of their exuberant performance during the months of autumn, bringing the season to a spectacular climax.

THE GENUS *SALVIA* INCLUDES many garden-worthy plants, some of which have show-off qualities. Sheets of *Salvia patens* are unrelentingly gorgeous, the dark green leaves conspiring with the ultramarine flowers to create drama with the hypnotic depth of a tropical sea. The detail of this Mexican sage is enthralling; each flower is an individual with a curious hood and long lower lip concealing mystery within. Associating clear cerulean blue *S. p.* 'Cambridge Blue' with *Cosmos atrosanguineus* and *Nicotiana langsdorffii* makes a sharp, exciting combination. The long, lime-green funnels of the tobacco plant are about the same tone as those of the salvia. Inside the bells, the anthers are blue, exactly the same blue as the salvia flowers. The large, velvety daisies of the chocolate cosmos, as close to black as any flower can be, complete the trio. All three plants are on the tender side. Both salvias and cosmos form tubers which in colder climes can be stored in the same way as dahlias (the cosmos is a very close relation). Growth of many of these Central and South American plants does not start until early summer. They may be late to rise but, once they get going, shoot up rapidly, giving their all and producing masses of colour until the frosts. They make excellent container subjects and may be happily potted and brought into growth under cover. The nicotiana may be raised from seed sown in winter.

Salvia guaranitica, especially its form 'Black and Blue', is an astonishing plant that can easily grow to 1.8–2.1m/6–7ft in a season. Its only drawback is that it may start to give a display of its magnificent, hooded, blue flowers, wrapped in their coal black bracts, as the first frosts start to bite. Normally, cutting back herbaceous plants early in the season is a device to make them flower later and at a lower level than they would otherwise do. In the case of *S. guaranitica*, taking out the apical shoot and cutting back the laterals to two or three nodes from the main branches not only ensures a shorter, bushier plant but also seems to induce early flower production. Seize any and every opportunity to maximize your enjoyment of these mysterious blooms.

Sometimes the quantity of a colour within one plant compels us to focus on it. Although a green-leaved canna can have show-stopping consequences on account of its scale, varieties with bronze foliage are the real show-offs. Not only are they immense, but the rich dark sienna of their scrolled leaves opening into giant paddles is in complete contrast to the verdancy of most gardens. When the great exotic clump is topped by spikes of orchid-like blooms of tropical fruit shades, nothing else gets a look in.

Cannas come from the Caribbean and South America but thrive all over the world where conditions suit them, in warmer climes often escaping the confines of the garden and naturalizing in the surrounding area. They are a typical example of the 'interpenetration of cultures', in this case of horticultures. In temperate climates they need a little more help. Rhizomes can be started off in pots of good, loam-based compost in spring and moved outside or planted directly from their winter resting place when danger of frost is past. When temperatures fall at the other end of the season and foliage

Right
The furry flowers of Salvia guaranitica *'Black and Blue' protrude from black bracts which intensify their impact.*

becomes tattered and blackened, they can be cut down, lifted and brought under cover, nestled snugly in old compost and politely ignored apart from a drop of water to prevent desiccation. Alternatively, if you want to increase your stocks throughout the winter, you can keep them growing with the minimum of heat and split off pieces of rhizome, potting them up individually.

Cannas are accommodating and generous plants, needing only sun and adequate moisture to thrive. Returns on such small investment are enormous. Few subjects can compare with their dramatic presence, although where they are planted in the garden and with whom makes all the difference. Drama can easily turn to farce. Cannas used as dot plants in municipal bedding schemes always look so lonely, like a scarecrow in a field of wheat. But associate the same plant with fellow flamboyants, either to battle for attention or just to raise the stakes, and it exhibits its true colours.

None more so than *Canna* 'Durban'. This is almost a caricature of a canna, a drama queen *par excellence*. Its magnificent, oval leaves drawn to a sharp, pinched point are deep, opulent purple, striped along the veins and parallel to them with rich raspberry pink. The midribs of the leaves and the stems are also pink, supporting, late in the season, flowers of unexpected brilliant orange. 'Garish and gaudy' some would say; 'glamorous and gorgeous' would come the reply. The flowers look like something from a magician's act, like the silken flags tucked into the crook of his hand. One tug and surely the flower would unfurl, followed by a stream of others in equally brilliant shades.

Like all good Thespians, cannas benefit from being well lit. Oblique light is best, giving the leaves a translucence not present when the sun is directly overhead. Strong, clear morning sunlight shines through the leaves, delineating midribs and veins and making the patterns of bi-coloured leaves even more clean-cut. As the sun goes down, a subtler, softer effect is created, colours glow and the shadows of other actors are revealed, silhouetted against the luminous leaves.

Hedychiums are closely related to cannas but hail from Asia and are tougher. Adventurous gardeners with reasonably sheltered gardens can try leaving the hardier species and their hybrids *in situ* in warm beds with rich soil. As long as the tubers don't freeze (the best protection is a mound of soil, although this can look like the scene of a mole invasion), they should spring into growth in early summer. Beware, though: nothing succeeds like success. Hedychiums are banned in New Zealand where their propensity to spread and colonize has become a serious threat to native species. In the temperate regions of the United States and Europe global warming has not yet reached the stage where we need worry too much about our ginger lilies making a break for it.

The asset hedychiums possess which cannas do not is perfume. Perfume is far too proper and restrained a word for it. As dusk descends their flowers exude the most exotic smell. Close your eyes and you could be in India, treading a dusty track warm with the accumulated heat from the long day's

Right

Most red hot pokers are striking. The great, flaming torches of Kniphofia rooperi *light up the autumn garden.*

sun, the sky ablaze with its fire as it exits over the blue silhouette of the mountains. Scent is the most evocative of all the senses, nowhere better than in the garden, and yet so seldom mentioned or considered – perhaps because it is the sense furthest away from words or intellect. Most hedychiums have it in abundance. *Hedychium gardnerianum* can have as many as thirty individual blossoms to a spike. The pale yellow flowers open in succession, pushing forward long, red stamens that blatantly broadcast their presence. Each bloom has the long corolla tube typical of flowers pollinated by moths. Jasmine and honeysuckle share the same characteristic and the same pale colouring also associated with nocturnal pollination. Flowers of the night.

Some plants employ both stature and psychedelic colour to grab our interest. The rocketing heads of *Kniphofia rooperi* head for the sky. Their ascent is rapid. From clumps of rather untidy leaves, pale, tightly packed buds appear in late summer. A few weeks later the stems which support them are 1.5m/5ft high. By now the buds have developed, green-tipped and lengthening by the day. As they shoot out from the stem in all directions the colour heats up until it blazes, vivid orange above and searingly bright yellow at the base. Red hot pokers indeed. Seen against a pure blue autumn sky, they make such a striking picture it is hard to drag yourself away.

At the same time of year some of the big North American daisies reach their peak. The individual flowers of *Helianthus* 'Lemon Queen' could never have the same impact as the fat torpedoes of *Kniphofia rooperi* but a huge waving clump of their soft yellow daisies is just as mesmerizing. If this plant likes you it will grow and grow, upwards and outwards. In fertile soil it can hold its own against any histrionics from the likes of cannas and dahlias.

Exotic does not necessarily mean tender. There are some really hardy plants that need no cosseting or careful handling to give a sterling performance every time. Although big, 'bowl-you-over' foliage is usually associated with jungle and tropical forest, some of the most startling leaves belong to plants from temperate climes.

The majestic leaves of *Rheum palmatum* 'Atrosanguineum', which comes from western China, could have stepped out of a Rousseau canvas. Nobody ever writes about its big, fat, round, shiny, pink buds which burst through the desiccated remnants of the bases of last year's leaf stalks with rude and urgent force. I have seen prim gardeners look away when they come across it lurking in the dank reaches of the springtime garden. Nothing else looks so shockingly new. Soon enough the buds unfurl into heavily veined leaves, dark crimson, crimped and corrugated like brains, broadening rapidly and held higher and higher aloft by stout, red stems. By the time these standards have reached their full height they are smooth and quite dry in texture. They have become greener but their undersides are still richly ruby red. Often they are so tall that you look up through the leaves rather than down on them and can fully appreciate their sumptuous colouring. But this plant does a double whammy. Without warning a stem appears rocketing upwards until, reaching way above

the head of the average gardener, it explodes into huge, fluffy feathers of deep cherry red. Who could look away now?

Dahlias originate from Mexico and Central America. Isn't it obvious? Obvious is the right word too. Dahlias do not know how to be subtle; their big, blatant flowers make a cacophony of colour and nobody can turn a blind ear to it. At one time gardeners of the subtle persuasion would not dream of growing dahlias. Too often they were outcasts confined to the allotments and vegetable patches of enthusiasts, many of whom grew dahlias exclusively for show. But, thanks to prestigious champions of the ilk of Christopher Lloyd (is anybody of the ilk of Christopher Lloyd?), dahlias have made a comeback. Although they have been begrudgingly accepted into garden society, they will never be regarded as respectable. Thank goodness.

The dahlia's appeal is direct. The red of *Dahlia* 'Bishop of Llandaff' is that of fresh blood. Opening in succession from late summer onwards, scores of flowers are set off by the strong, bronze foliage which embellishes the plant's sturdy growth. To show off it needs subtle companions – tall *Molinia*, *Cotinus* 'Grace' or the grey leaves of *Elaeagnus* 'Quicksilver'. Sometimes it is more exciting, though, to let it do battle. Confronting the tall, lime green heads of *Euphorbia palustris* or *E. schillingii,* it is at its ostentatious best: the green is more vividly acidic, the red more blatantly red. Mix in a few *Crocosmia* 'Lucifer', light the blue touch paper and retire.

The Bishop has become a popular plant, but there are hundreds of other dahlias which deserve a chance to enter the mainstream of our gardening consciousness. Of those with bronze foliage, *Dahlia* 'David Howard' is one of the best. It produces soft orange, double flowers in profusion and, although not as ostentatious as some, is always arresting. The single *D.* 'Moonfire' has a more yellow background colour and has rings of orange and red around the central disc. It is lovely with some of the hot-toned achilleas and with *Stipa arundinacea* in olive and orange, throwing up its mobile stems at random and creating ribbons of underlying colour.

Dahlias are a knockout. Nothing is more vivacious. Their vivid flowers bring the sound of a *mariachi* band right into the flowerbed. Some drama queens, however, are more subtle, although the final result is just as prepossessing. The allure of *Angelica gigas* is quiet at first. It is only when the stems reach a towering 1.8m/6ft and the fat buds burst asunder, revealing platforms of the darkest crimson flowers, that their true impact is felt. In their infancy they are often consumed by snails. Perhaps like *A. archangelica*, whose stems have been used in confectionery for centuries, *A. gigas* tastes delicious. Certainly it is used extensively in Chinese medicine. Just looking at it does me good. It has power and majesty and enormous charisma.

Another dark-leaved angelica, *A. sylvestris* 'Vicar's Mead', has almost black, pinnate leaves. In flower it makes as big a plant as *A. gigas* but the inflorescence is an interesting, mucky-pink. I know that it is delicious at least to Highland cattle, three of whom devoured a plant each when they visited my

Right

Strange and exciting, the earthy-red buds of Lobelia tupa *project from the stems like birds craning their necks. The lower flower petals protrude, exposing the stigma.*

garden without invitation one June day. *Angelica pachycarpa* has some of the shiniest foliage around. The leaves are deep green and catch the colour of the sky on their reflective surface. They are huge, especially when growing in damp, fertile soil, which seems to suit all the species in this most remarkable group. The lime green umbels are magnificent too, but there is always an element of sadness about their arrival since all these plants are monocarpic and, having set seed, die. Life span can be extended by taking out the flower stems immediately after they finish flowering.

The shape and bearing of the flowers of *Lobelia tupa* from Chile are reminiscent of Mayan and Inca sculptural forms. This perennial plant looks more like a shrub. It makes strong, upright growth with a forest of bronze stems dressed with grey, furry leaves, terminating in flowers of an earthy red. There may be as many as forty or fifty flowers to each stem creating a bottle-brush effect. Each individual flower is held separately on its own stem, pushing out its lower petal in an exaggerated way like a rude tongue. It is hard to say whether there are several slender petals which join at their extremity or whether there is one petal slashed at intervals. Above this arrangement the long style rears, its sticky stigma ready and waiting for the attentions of the next hummingbird. Dusted with pollen from earlier forays, the birds hover, dipping their tongues deep into the flower to collect nectar, and simultaneously transfer pollen to the stigma. This clever pollination process results in a flower which looks like an ancient bird mask, startling and exciting.

Most drama queens are big. But if you are feisty enough, size is not important. *Crocosmia* achieve a dramatic effect through sheer weight of numbers: there are several flowers to each stem and there are stems *ad infinitum*. They make new rhizomes constantly, one on top of the other like strings of big, bold beads. Each new tuber may send out several new shoots, like a sputnik, and each of these will eventually become a new tuber. No wonder they move so fast, increasing exponentially. Complaining about the invasive nature of *Crocosmia*, especially of montbretia (*C.* x *crocosmiiflora*), is a gardener's favourite pastime, but in a naturalistic planting fluid swathes of the best hybrids are ideal among legions of *Rudbeckia*, *Helenium* and *Achillea*. *Crocosmia* establishes its presence early in the year when broad blades of pale, translucent green spring up amongst other emerging foliage to catch the limelight at the first opportunity. Its swords keep apace with the surrounding rush of growth, lengthening and becoming more substantial. Within the leaves, buds start to fatten up, emerging eventually in their own right as the summer progresses and swiftly spreading their wildfire all around. *Crocosmia* 'Lucifer' is one of the biggest and best, with great, pleated leaves and fiery-red flowers borne on tall, branching stems. At Glebe Cottage we have a vivid red *Crocosmia*, strong and stocky, which we have called 'Flame' – it lights up my flowerbeds with its dramatic intensity.

Whether they are fiery red, rich yellow or flaming orange, drama is the *raison d'être* for *Crocosmia* – they are impossible to ignore. Herbaceous

Potentilla produce masses of flowers too – and flagrant ones to boot. *Potentilla* 'William Rollison', for instance, with its big orange, yellow and vermilion flowers, and extra petals just to over-state the case, can really turn up the volume in a quiet display. *Potentilla* 'Gibson's Scarlet' can have the same effect, although it makes noise by the sheer saturated red of its flowers. It employs no sophistry, just blatant colour shock.

All these small-flowered members of the rose family qualify as drama queens because of the volume and vibrancy of their massed flower power. There are a few plants, though, which join the free-for-all despite their flowers and entirely on account of their leaves. Foliage gives a more sustained performance than flowers and there are other ways of grabbing the limelight than employing psychedelic colour. Groovy baby! *Melianthus major* has some of the most dramatic of all foliage. In the wild in South Africa it is an evergreen shrub. In all but the kindest climates of North America and Europe it behaves like a herbaceous plant. If its top growth is left *in situ* till spring frosts are over to protect imminent new growth, the old damaged stems can then be cut to their base. In one season new growth can attain up to 2.4m/8ft. At the height of its magnificence it stops people in their tracks, demanding recognition of its celebrity status. The grey-green leaves are deeply cut and serrated as though trimmed by a giant's pinking shears. Each leaf is poised along the stem and each stem is perfectly juxtaposed with the next. Unmistakably A-list!

With drama queens around there may be discord or even violent conflicts as they vie with one another for our attention. But one good clash is worth a hundred boring harmonies. And one thing is for sure – when these brazen beauties make their presence felt, garden life will never be dull.

A–Z of plants

These plants appear in the main text, but the list below provides simple information about heights, habits, most suitable sites and special conditions or treatment they might need. It does not purport to be comprehensive but it gives basic information and offers a starting point for anyone not acquainted with particular plants.

Acanthus spinosus
Spiny bear's breeches. Height up to 1.5m/5ft. Handsome, shiny leaves set with spines. A. s. Spinosissimus Group is even more heavily armed. Very invasive. Sun. More willing to flower in poorer soil. Z4

Achillea millefolium
Yarrow. Height 60cm/2ft. Large, flat flower heads on strong stems. New hybrids appear every year. Full sun and good drainage (short-lived in wet soil). Z5

Agapanthus
Nile lily. Height 30–90cm/1–3ft. Drumstick heads of lily-like flowers. A. 'Blue Mist' is tall and pale blue. 'Midnight' is small with very deep blue flowers. Full sun and rich soil. Grow large-leaved evergreen varieties in pots and over-winter under cover. Protect crowns of deciduous varieties from severe frost. Z5–7

Anchusa azurea 'Loddon Royalist'
Borage. Height up to 1m/3ft. Short-lived perennial. Vivid, ultramarine flowers. Prefers deep, silty soil where its tap roots establish well. Sun. Must be propagated by root cuttings. Plants from seed sold under this name do not compare. Z5

Anemone nemorosa
Wood anemone. Height 10cm/4in. Dainty, white flowers with pink reverse, finely cut foliage. Many selections in pink and blue and several with quirky forms. Colonizes freely in humus-rich woodland conditions. Flowers in spring. Summer dormant. Z4

Anemonella thalictroides
Rue anemone. Height 15cm/6in. Tiny, white or pink flowers, occasionally green, sometimes with extra petals, rarely fully double. Humus-rich woodland conditions. Early and tough. Z4

Angelica gigas
Height up to 1.8m/6ft. Enormous biennial umbellifer. Green growth changes dramatically to crimson as flowering begins. A. sylvestris 'Vicar's Mead' has dark maroon foliage and branching stems terminating in dusty-pink flowers. A. pachycarpa is shorter (1m/3ft), with shiny leaves and greenish flowers. Moisture-retentive soil. Sun or dappled shade. Z4

Aquilegia longissima
Columbine. Height 45cm/18in. Elegant, pale yellow flowers with immense spurs. A. chrysantha is similar. A. vulgaris and A. alpina are long-lived and the parents of A. 'Hensol Harebell' with wide, elegant flowers and making stately clumps. Best in substantial soil and dappled shade. Z5

Arisaema consanguineum
Height up to 1.2m/4ft. Unusual aroid with urn-shaped spathe with long tail. Leaves held like an upturned umbrella above flower. Sun or shade. Z7

Artemisia 'Powis Castle'
Wormwood. Height 1m/3ft. Finely cut, silvery leaves. Makes a strong bush and wastes no energy producing flowers. Full sun and well-drained soil. Prune hard in spring. A. schmidtiana 'Nana' is tiny (15cm/6in) and ideal for carpeting the ground in a sunny spot. Z5

Arum italicum subsp. italicum 'Marmoratum'
Lords and ladies. Cuckoo pint. Height 45cm/18in. Rich green, arrow-shaped leaves are marked strongly with white in winter. Green spathes produced in late spring are followed by columns of glossy, orange red berries. Z6

Asarum europaeum
Wild ginger. Height 15cm/6in. Very shiny leaves and insignificant greenish flowers. Prefers shade and humus-rich soil. Z6

Aster cordifolius 'Little Carlow'
Selection of common blue wood aster. Height 1m/3ft. Arresting clouds of blue on strong stems. Attractive to butterflies. A. divaricatus is shorter (45cm/18in) with white daisies on arching stems and glossy, dark green leaves. Sun or part shade. Good soil. A. lateriflorus 'Horizontalis' (60cm/2ft), with tiny flowers on horizontal laterals and small, dark leaves, prefers full sun and fertile soil, decently drained. Z3

Aster x frikartii 'Mönch'
Height up to 1.5m/5ft. Strong stems support a succession of large, single, blue daisies with long, narrow petals and green centres, becoming yellow. Easy-going but responds to good cultivation, fertile soil and sun. Z5

Astrantia major
Masterwort. Height 45cm/18in. Long-flowering, tolerant plants with papery bracts and a mass of quivering stamens. Many new crimson varieties. Damp soil in sun or shade. Z3

Campanula lactiflora
Milky bellflower. Height 1.5m/5ft. Tall, branching stems laden with clouds of open bellflowers in pale blue and white. C. l. 'Loddon Anna' is pale lilac. Good soil. Open border or dappled shade. Z4

Campanula 'Sarastro'
Height 75cm/30in. Spreading plant producing straight stems laden with big, blue, waxy bells. Good soil. Sun or shade. Z5

Campanula latifolia
Greater bellflower. Height 1m/3ft. Long, blue bells. Dappled shade and humus-rich soil. Self-seeds. Z4

Campanula persicifolia
Peach-leaved bellflower. Height 45cm/18in. Evergreen basal growth.

Straight stems bear large bells of blue or white. Many esoteric forms, including doubles and cup-in-cup. Sun or dappled shade. Easy-going. Z4

Canna indica
Indian shot. Height 1.2m/4ft. Large, paddle-shaped leaves and red flowers. Hybrids have showy flowers and big leaves, some bronze or striped, some taller, others more dwarf. C. 'Durban' has particularly ornamental foliage. Must be lifted and stored in all but frost-free gardens. Z8

Chaerophyllum hirsutum 'Roseum'
Hairy chervil. Height 1m/3ft. Rich green, ferny leaves, dark stems and lilac pink flowers in umbels. Any soil that is neither waterlogged nor very dry. Does well in shade. Z4

Chamerion angustifolium 'Album'
Rosebay willow-herb. Height 1.2m/4ft. Strong stems clad with narrow leaves. Open spikes of green and white flowers. Gentle pink with red calyces in C. a. 'Stahl Rose'. Very invasive. Will grow anywhere. Z5

Cirsium rivulare 'Atropurpureum'
Brook thistle. Height 1.2m/4ft. Crimson thistles on tall stems. Damp, fertile ground. Sun or dappled shade. Z5

Colchicum autumnale
Naked ladies. Height up to 30cm/1ft. Globe-shaped flowers in autumn without leaves. Spring foliage disappears before the flowers. Z4

Cortaderia selloana
Pampas grass. Height 1.8–3.6m/6–12ft. Statuesque. Fluffy, silken heads carried in late autumn. 'Pumila' is more compact. Open situation. Any

soil, though best in damp, fertile ground. Z7

Corydalis flexuosa
Fumitory. Height 30cm/1ft. Spread 60cm/2ft. Ferny leaves, usually bronze-tinged; long-spurred, blue flowers. Distinct selections include C. f. 'Père David', 'China Blue' and 'Purple Leaf'. C. elata is taller (up to 45cm/18in), leaves larger and more rounded. All like damp, leafy soil under deciduous trees. Z4

Cosmos atrosanguineus
Chocolate plant. Height 60cm/2ft. Dark, velvety flowers like single dahlias to which it is closely related. Chocolate scent on warm days. Fertile soil and full sun. Z8

Cotinus 'Grace'
Smoke bush. Height 1.8m/6ft plus. Shrub with round, maroon leaves. Flowers are fine and wispy. Excellent foil for vivid red flowers. Good soil and sun. Z5

Crambe cordifolia
Greater sea kale. Height 1.8m/6ft. Intricately branched, green stems decorated with thousands of scented, white flowers followed by bead-like fruit. Best in full sun and good depth of fertile soil. Z6

Crocosmia
Height 60cm/2ft. Spreading, rhizomatous perennial. Sword-like leaves and slender stems. Lily-like flowers in vibrant oranges, reds and yellows. 'Lucifer' is much taller with pleated leaves and open, branching stems of vivid red flowers. 'Flame' is short with vermilion flowers. Z6

Cyclamen hederifolium
Ivy-leaved cyclamen. Height 10cm/4in. Tuberous-rooted perennial, summer dormant. Leaves and flowers appear in

midwinter. C. coum is similar with plainer and more rounded leaves. Z5

Dahlia
Height up to 1.2m/4ft. Tender, tuberous rooted perennials. Exotic flowers in rich colours at their peak in late summer and autumn. Classified by size and flower shape. Z9

Deschampsia flexuosa
Wavy hair grass. Height 45cm–2m/18in–6ft. Many garden forms. All prefer damp, heavy ground. Shade or sun. Z4

Digitalis parviflora
Bronze foxglove. Height 1m/3ft. Tall, close spires of furry, brown bells followed by shiny, columnar seed heads. Will cope with most situations. Prefers well-drained soil. Z5

Dracunculus vulgaris
Dragon arum. Height 75cm/30in. Spotted stems and arrow-shaped leaves support dark spathes. Emits unpleasant smell until pollinated (by bluebottles). Z8

Echinacea purpurea
Purple coneflower. Height 75cm/30in. Pink daisies with raised bronze centres. In E. p. 'White Swan' the petals are greenish white. Full sun in an open position. Fertile soil. Z5

Echinops ritro
Globe thistle. Height 1.5m/5ft. Spherical, silver heads changing to blue. E. r. subsp. ruthenicus is a superior variety. E. tournefortii is taller with white flowers. Well-drained soil and full sun promote flower production and quality. Z4

Elaeagnus 'Quicksilver'
Height up to 1.8m/6ft. Deciduous, suckering shrub. Silvery foliage a telling

backdrop for tall, herbaceous plants. Flowers, with sweet scent, in early summer. Sun and well-drained soil. Z5

Epimedium x versicolor 'Neosulphureum'
Spiderwort. Barrenwort. Height 40cm/16in. Spread 75cm/30in. Glossy, evergreen, ovate leaves, often burnished in winter. Dainty, pale yellow flowers. Copes well with dry shade. E. davidii and E. accuminatum need leafy soil and protection from cold winds. E. grandiflorum is best in dappled shade but can cope with an open situation if the soil is humus-rich. Cut back old foliage before growth starts in spring. Z5

Eryngium alpinum
Sea holly. Height 60cm/2ft. Branching flower heads. Bracts soft and much divided. Can be raised from fresh seed (select the bluest, fuzziest flowers). Sun and well-drained soil. E. bourgatii is shorter (45cm/18in), with branching stems and large, bracted flower cones. Seems to appreciate fertile soil. Z5

Eryngium giganteum
Miss Wilmott's ghost. Height 1.5m/5ft. Biennial. Rosettes of round, leathery leaves from which rise, in the second year, tall, branching stems with big 'sea holly' heads, grey-green becoming silvery-white. Heavily barbed. Loves sun. Self-seeds profusely. Z6

Erythronium californicum
Trout lily. Height 25cm/10in. Elegant, lily-like flowers in pale pink or white on arching stems. E. tuolumnense is taller (30cm/1ft) with yellow turkscap flowers and fresh green leaves, sometimes marbled. Summer dormant. Damp soil in a sheltered position. Z5

Erythronium dens-canis
Dog's tooth violet. Height 10cm/4in. Flowers pink, gently reflexed. Broad basal leaves often marbled. Dappled shade. Z3

Euphorbia palustris
Marsh spurge. Height 1m/3ft. Fresh green foliage and heads of lime yellow bracts. Good autumn colour. E. schillingii is similar with more handsome, broader foliage. Damp, heavy soil. Sun or dappled shade. Z5

Francoa ramosa
Bridal wreath. Height 60cm/2ft. Copious, evergreen rosettes, burnished in the winter. Slender stems bear up to 50 flowers. White-flowered forms are particularly susceptible to frost and need winter protection. F. sonchifolia Rogerson's form with magenta flowers is one of the toughest and most distinctive. Z7

Fritillaria meleagris
Snakeshead fritillary. Height 25cm/10in. Slender foliage and pendulous bells tessellated in purple, or occasionally pure white. Loves damp ground and can cope with flooding. Colonizes by self-seeding. Z3

Fritillaria verticillata
Height 12–14in/30–35cm. Subtle green bells with maroon markings. Plant bulbs deeply in damp soil in dappled shade. F. camschatcensis likes damp conditions, whereas statuesque F. persica 'Adiyaman' and F. imperialis prefer sun and good drainage. Z5

Galactites tomentosa
Mediterranean thistle. Height 45cm/18in. Biennial. Spiny, branching bushes with small, pink thistles. Z6

Galanthus nivalis
Snowdrop. Height 15cm/6in. Pure white, pendulous flowers tipped with green. Slender, upright foliage. More than 100 varieties. Heavy, moist soil. Increases well. Z4

Gaura lindheimeri
Height 1m/3ft. Small, spotted leaves on willowy stems. Top third wreathed in delicate flowers, white with a touch of pink. 'Siskyou Pink' is a shorter, pink-flowered version. Sun. Moist in summer, but fairly dry in winter. Z6

Gillenia trifoliata
Bowman's root. Height 75cm/30in. Open, branching habit with dainty leaves and even daintier, white flowers. Russet autumn colour. Good, humus-rich soil. Sun or dappled shade. Z5

Geranium pratense
Meadow cranesbill. Height 75cm/30in. Easy geranium with single and double forms ranging in colour from blue through lilac and pink to white. Any soil. Self-seeds. Z5

Geranium psilostemon
Armenian cranesbill. Height 1m/3ft. Vivid magenta flowers with coal-black centres. 'Ann Folkard' has trailing growth with yellow foliage. Both tolerant of a variety of conditions but best in an open, sunny site. Good on heavy soils. Z4

Gladiolus papilio
Purpureoauratus Group
Height 75cm/30in. Subtly coloured flowers. Narrow, glaucous, sword-like leaves. Loves baking sun and excellent drainage. Increase by dividing corms in spring. Z7

Gunnera manicata
Giant rhubarb. Height 1.8m/6ft. Immense, coarse rhubarb leaves on thick, prickly stems. Damp, heavy soil in full sun. Z7

Hedychium gardnerianum
Ginger lily. Height up to 1.8m/6ft. Broad, elegant leaves wrapped around straight, strong stems. Night-scented flowers. Any reasonable soil. Prefers sun. Lift and store in all but frost-free gardens. Z8

Helenium autumnale
Sneezeweed. Height 60cm–1.2m/2–4ft. Straightforward daisies with raised doorknob centres surrounded by a circle of petals. H. 'Moerheim Beauty' is bronze, 'Summer Circle' yellow. Full sun, good soil. Z5

Helianthus 'Lemon Queen'
Perennial sunflower. Height up to 1.8m/6ft. Strong, spreading sunflower with copious, pale yellow, black-centred flowers. Any soil which does not dry out. Sun. Split clumps every two years. Z5

Helleborus × hybridus
Lenten rose. Height 40cm/16in. Long-lived, evergreen perennial. Large, palmate leaves and a multitude of substantial flowers in colours ranging from black to white. Best in shade. Z4

Hordeum jubatum
Barley grass. Height 45cm/18in. Perennial grass with barley heads with long awns. Any soil. Open situation in sun. Z6

Hosta (Tardiana Group) 'Halcyon'
Funkia. Plantain lily. Height 45cm/18in. Large, glaucous-blue leaves of exquisite shape. Substantial soil. Prefers dappled shade (grey-leaved varieties can cope with sun). Feed and mulch with organic matter frequently. Z4

Imperata cylindrica 'Rubra'
Blood grass. Height 37cm/15in. Blades start green but quickly change to crimson. Gently running habit. Good soil. Sun. Divide in spring. Z6

Iris chrysographes
Height 45cm/18in. Narrow leaves, branching flower stems with slender, pointed buds. Black form has almost black flowers, sumptuous and velvety. Moist soil in sun. Z4

Iris 'Rajah'
Bearded iris. Height 60cm/2ft. All bearded irises, many descended from I. fiorentina, love sun and poor soil. Expose rhizomes to ripen them and improve flower production. Z5

Iris reticulata
Netted iris. Height 10cm/4in. Numerous hybrids of this and I. histriodes. Deep planting essential. Z5

Iris unguicularis
Algerian iris. Height 30cm/1ft. Perfumed winter iris. Needs sun and shelter to produce showy, purple flowers. Selections include 'Mary Barnard' (deep purple) and 'Walter Butt' (pale lavender-grey and particularly good scent). Z8

Jeffersonia diphylla
Twin leaf. Height 25cm/10in. Leaves in pairs at the top of tall stems. Single, white flowers on their own stems. J. dubia has soft lavender-blue flowers and purple-tinged, heart-shaped leaves. Canopy shade and shelter. Z4

Knautia macedonica
Height 45cm/18in. Crimson pincushion flowers for months. Sun and well-drained soil. Z5

Kniphofia rooperi
Red hot poker. Height up to 1.8m/6ft. Majestic, with

huge, red and yellow flower spikes late in the season. Good soil, ample moisture and sun. Z6

Lamium orvala
Dead nettle. Height 75cm/30in. Dusty-pink flowers held in whorls around erect stems under rings of leaves. Deep soil in sun or dappled shade. Z4

Leucojum aestivum
Summer snowflake. Height 60cm/2ft. Nodding, white flowers with green tips on erect stems. One of the few bulbs that thrives in wet ground. Z4

Lobelia tupa
Devil's tobacco. Height up to 1.8m/6ft. Herbaceous but makes a big, shrubby plant each summer. Grey-green leaves and strange, brick-red flowers. Prefers deep, moist soil and full sun. Z7

Lunaria annua
Honesty. Height 60cm/2ft. Biennial with rich purple, crucifer flowers followed by flat, silvery discs that persist for months. Self-seeds. Foliage of L a. 'Alba Variegata' is splashed boldly with white. White flowers. Z6

Meconopsis betonicifolia
Blue Himalayan poppy. Height 60cm/2ft (taller when growing well). Usually monocarpic. M. grandis is similar but perennial. M. punicea is a red-flowered relation. Moist, cool conditions. Dappled shade and humus-rich soil with leaf mould incorporated. Z3

Melianthus major
Honey bush. Height 1.2m/4ft. Shrub usually treated as a herbaceous subject in all but the mildest gardens. Large, toothed, glaucous leaves. Well-drained soil. Sun. Z9

Melica uniflora
Wood mellick. Height 30–60cm/1–2ft. Gently spreading grass for shade. Good in a dry site. Prefers alkaline conditions. Z5

Melittis melissophyllum
Bastard balm. Height 45cm/18in. Leafy clumps with numerous stems. Hooded, white or pink flowers in whorls. Tolerates changing light and moisture levels. Dappled shade and leafy soil. Z4

Molinia caerulea
Blue moor grass. Height 75cm–1.8m/30in–6ft. Wistful grass with dainty, well-spaced flowers. Growth green, purple and blue changing to rich, biscuity hues as winter sets in. Open site in soil which does not dry out. Z5

Nepeta govaniana
Catmint. Height 60cm/2ft. Airy, branching plant with wiry stems, soft, aromatic foliage and a scattering of tiny, creamy-white, hooded flowers. Rich, damp soil. Sun or dappled shade. Z5

Nicotiana langsdorfii
Tobacco plant. Height 60cm/2ft. Lime green, narrow, tubular flowers, flaring at their extremity. Raise from seed sown early in the year. Prick out and pot on, planting out when frost is past. Z8

Omphalodes linifolia
Venus's navelwort. Height 30cm/1ft. Annual. Glaucous leaves and hundreds of small, white flowers. Needs excellent drainage and full sun. Z6

Onopordon acanthium
Scotch thistle. Height 1.5m/5ft. Self-sowing biennial. Branching, shoulder-high stems with large, spiky, purple thistles. Z6

Orlaya grandiflora
Height 45cm/18in. Very decorative biennial. Gently branching plant bearing a series of creamy-white umbels edged by large, sterile petals. Easily grown from seed started under cover in modules. Z7

Paeonia mlokosewitschii
Peony. Height 75cm/30in. Ephemeral, lemon petals arranged in globes. Glaucous early foliage and fat buds. Most species peonies relish fertile soil in sun or dappled shade. Z5

Papaver orientale
Oriental poppy. Height 45cm–1.5m/18in–5ft. Huge flowers with wavy petals in a wealth of glorious colours, all with dark centres. Good drainage and full sun. Z4

Papaver somniferum
Opium poppy. Height 90cm/3ft. Glaucous stems, leaves and seed heads. Masses of flamboyant, ephemeral flowers in a wide range of colours and forms. Self-seeds. Z7

Paris polyphylla
Height up to 1.2m/4ft. Asiatic woodlander. Needs a shady, humus-rich site. Mark the planting site well – paris goes to bed early and gets up late. Z5

Patrinia scabiosifolia
Height 1.2m/4ft. Tall, straight stems, branching at their tops and bearing large heads composed of tiny, citric yellow flowers. Scabious-like leaves turn red and russet in autumn. Any reasonably drained soil in sun. Self-seeds. Z6

Pennisetum alopecuroides 'Herbstzauber' (Autumn Magic)
Fountain grass. Height 45cm/18in. Late-flowering and best in warmer gardens, this needs sunshine and good drainage. Cut back and divide in spring. Z6

Podophyllum peltatum
Mayapple. Height 60cm/2ft. Woodlander that shoots into life mid-spring. Two umbrella-like leaves with a single, white flower on top are followed by a large, red berry. P. hexandrum is shorter (45cm/18in) than P. peltatum. Exciting foliage and single, pink flower. Both relish deep leaf mould. Z5

Polemonium caeruleum
Jacob's ladder. Height 45cm/18in. Stiff stems are headed by clumps of blue flowers. Good sterile hybrids include P. 'Lambrook Mauve', 'Glebe Cottage Lilac' and 'Bressingham Purple'. Prefers a site in sun and moist soil. Z5

Potentilla
Cinquefoil. Height 45cm/18in. P. atrosanguinea has red to deep crimson flowers. Numerous named hybrids, mostly sterile and long-lived, include 'William Rollison' (flashy, orange-yellow flowers with extra petals) and 'Gibson's Scarlet' (vivid blood-red flowers). P. x hopwoodiana (strawberries-and-cream flowers) is shorter (30cm/1ft). All like good soil and sun. Z5

Primula bulleyana
Candelabra primula. Height 60cm/2ft. Upright stems with whorls of orange flowers. Big rosettes of leaves which vanish by late summer. Damp, heavy ground. Z5

Primula sieboldii
Japanese primula. Height 15cm/6in. Much selected to produce a wide range of both colour and form. Increases well, especially in damp ground. Z4

Primula vulgaris
Primrose. Height 10cm/4in. Pale lemon flowers are borne

above rich green, crinkled leaves. Spring. The parent of hundreds of hybrids, including old Elizabethan doubles through to the ubiquitous modern polyanthus. All prefer a site in dappled shade and humus-rich soil. Divide frequently. Z4

Pulsatilla vulgaris
Pasque flower. Height 15cm/6in. Finely cut foliage and purple chalices of flowers. Stems, leaves, flowers and seed heads covered in fine, soft hair. Best in poor, sunny sites. Z4

Ranunculus aconitifolius 'Flore Pleno'
Bachelor's buttons, fair maids of France. Height 45cm/18in. Fully double pom-poms on wiry, branching stems in late spring. Damp, leafy soil. Z4

Rheum palmatum 'Atrosanguineum'
Ornamental rhubarb. Enormous leaves, crimson on the reverse, and towering flower spikes up to 1.8m/6ft. Tough and easy. Prefers heavy soil. Happy in sun or shade. Z5

Rodgersia pinnata 'Superba'
Height up to 1.2m/4ft. Bold, palmate leaves and heads of fluffy, pink flowers; bronze seed heads. Great autumn colour. R. podophylla is shorter (60cm/2ft), with white flowers. Rich, damp ground. Z5

Romneya coulteri
Californian tree poppy. Height 1.5m/5ft. Much-divided, glaucous foliage. Gigantic, white flowers with quivering, golden anthers. Well-drained soil (sandy and dry is best). Full sun. Z7

Rudbeckia fulgida var. deamii
Black-eyed Susan. Height 1m/3ft. Prairie daisy with bright yellow flowers that have raised, black central cones. Full sun. Fertile soil. 'Goldsturm' is very similar to this variety but shorter (45cm/18in). Z4

Rudbeckia maxima
Height 1.5m/5ft. Drooping, yellow petals, dark cone centre and glaucous, paddle-shaped leaves. Full sun and good soil. Z5

Salvia aethiopis
Mediterranean sage. Height 90cm/3ft. Biennial or short-lived perennial. Basal rosettes of grey, furry leaves and tall, branching spikes of small, hooded, white flowers. S. argentea is similar. Good drainage and full sun. Z6

Salvia patens
Blue sage. Height 60cm/2ft. Bushy habit with large, hooded, ultramarine flowers. S. p. 'Cambridge Blue' has cerulean blue flowers. Lift and store the tuberous roots over winter. Z7

Salvia guaranitica
Height 1.5m/5ft. Fresh green leaves with heads of small, rich blue flowers. S. g. 'Black and Blue' is taller with bigger flowers, deep blue with black bracts. Tuberous roots need protection in cold areas. Z8

Sanguinaria canadensis
Bloodroot. Height 20cm/8in. Single, white, ephemeral flowers, clasped by two leaves. Succulent, glaucous foliage with scalloped edges. S. c. f. multiplex is fully double and lasts a little longer. Z4

Scabiosa atropurpurea
Black scabious. Height 40cm/16in. Pincushion flowers on erect, bushy plants. Sun and well-drained soil. Z6

Schizostylis coccinea f. alba
South African lily. Height 45cm/18in. White-flowered form. Slender, upright leaves and stems. S. c. 'Major' has big, red, lustrous flowers and is very vigorous. 'Jennifer' has soft pink, rounded flowers. All varieties clump up fast in rich, damp ground in sun. Z6

Selinum wallichianum
Himalayan parsley. Height 1.5m/5ft. Long-lived perennial with finely cut foliage and umbels of creamy-white flowers. Deep loam suits it best but it grows well in any substantial, fertile soil including clay. Sun. Z4

Stipa gigantea
Spanish oats. Height 1.8m/6ft. From untidy clumps of basal foliage rise tall stems with oat-like flowers. S. arundinacea (tress grass) is shorter (60cm/2ft), fountain-like with orange and olive blades and see-through, pinkish inflorescences. S. tenuissima is shorter still (45cm/18in), with fine, soft blades and even softer biscuity inflorescences. Best in a well-drained, sunny site. Z6

Stachys byzantina
Lambs' lugs. Height 37cm/15in. Mats of thickly furry, silver leaves with fluffy flower spikes. Excellent ground cover. Thrives in dry, poor ground but will make itself at home in any well-drained, sunny site. Z5

Thalictrum delavayi
Chinese meadow rue. Height up to 1.8m/6ft. Fine, branching sprays of tiny, lavender flowers with pendulous, cream anthers over maidenhair. Good soil which does not dry out. Sun or partial shade. Z4

Tricyrtis formosana
Toad lily. Height up to 60cm/2ft. Autumn-flowering woodlander for humus-rich, shady site. Divide every two years. Keep stolons covered with mulch to help flower production. Z5

Trillium chloropetalum
Wakerobin. Height 15cm/6in. Spring woodlander (summer dormant) with leaves, petals and stamens in threes. Large, mottled bracts. T. grandiflorum has green bracts and pure white flowers. T. rivale is dainty. Leafy soil and dappled shade for all. Z4

Verbascum bombyciferum
Woolly mullein. Aaron's rod. Height up to 1.5m/5ft. Furry, silver leaves. Yellow flowers. Dry, sunny site. Self-sows. V. olympicum is taller (up to 2.4m/8ft). 'Cotswold King' is outstanding. All can be grown from seed. All relish alkaline soils. Z6

Verbena bonariensis
Argentinian vervain. Height 1.8m/6ft. Branching stems with masses of small flower heads composed of many tiny, purple flowers with brown bracts. Loves good drainage and sun. Self-seeds freely (banned in parts of Australia). Z8

Veronica gentianoides
Speedwell. Height 45cm/18in. Slender columns of intricately marked, pale blue flowers rise above evergreen rosettes which carpet the ground. Reasonable soil. Dappled shade or sun. Increase by division in spring, replanting outside rosettes 15cm/6in apart. Z4

Index

Page numbers in **bold italic** refer to the captions to photographs

Author's acknowledgements for the first edition

Thank you to Jonathan Buckley for his outstanding photographs. His industry and quest for perfection, tempered with consistent good humour, have made our collaboration an enormous pleasure.

Thanks to our editor Erica Hunningher for all her care, encouragement and finesse.

I am grateful to Simon Daley for his elegant design.

Thanks to Neil, my lovely husband, for believing this book would be written, and making sure it was, and to our daughters Annie and Alice for all their help, encouragement and optimism.

My gardening friends present and departed who come to life in my garden have helped more than they will ever know. Special thanks to Tom Fischer, editor of *Horticulture* magazine, for reading these words and making me feel he enjoyed them.

Most of all, thanks to the plants themselves and for the privilege of growing them. Whatever their personality, they are an inspiration to us all.

Photographer's acknowledgements

While the majority of the plant portraits were taken at Carol's garden at Glebe Cottage in Devon, I would like to thank all the other garden owners who allowed me to photograph in their gardens, in particular Sue and Wol Staines for their patience and enthusiasm in wading through Carol's ever-burgeoning lists of favourite plants and pointing me in the direction of their own fine specimens.

I would also like to thank the following garden owners whose gardens appear in the book as chapter openers: Christopher Lloyd, Great Dixter, East Sussex (pages 58, 140 and 150); Sarah Raven, Perch Hill, East Sussex (page 74); Sue and Wol Staines, Glen Chantry, Essex (pages 8 and 88).